JOY IS MY
MIDDLE NAME

Sasha Debevec-McKenney's poems have appeared in *The New Yorker*, the *New York Review of Books* and the *Yale Review*. She was the 2020-2021 Jay C. and Ruth Halls Poetry Fellow at the University of Wisconsin and is currently a creative writing fellow at Emory University. She was born in Hartford, Connecticut, and lives in Madison, Wisconsin.

'*Joy Is My Middle Name* is a mantra, motto, and winking forewarning in this magnificent debut. Humor is juxtaposed with heartbreak; the weird tenderness of an "ankle break support group on Facebook" is juxtaposed with civil war amputees. August Wilson, Jenny Holzer, and Amish girls make cameos. A poet with the capacious charms and chops of Sasha Debevec-McKenney comes around once a generation or so: Morgan Parker, Wanda Coleman, Frank O'Hara. *Joy Is My Middle Name* is bold as hell. It's revitalizing.'
— Terrance Hayes, author of *American Sonnet for My Past and Future Assassin*

'I've been itching to read Sasha Debevec-McKenney's debut for years—and boy, does this work of staggering bathos ever deliver. *Joy Is My Middle Name* is so horny and hilarious that you might not notice at first the incisive political critique propelling every poem, skewering every last shred of American culture from Costco and the death penalty to diet sodas and action movie franchises. I can't think of a book that zips more nimbly between the quotidian and the historic, or whose paratactic zingers better capture the weirdness of our age: "My chicken sandwich was dry. I was thirteen and this was the third Al Franken book I'd read", "My backyard is literally a lake. / I literally need a hug. I literally got a master's degree and felt nothing". What other book combines wart removal with Eleanor Roosevelt? Where else can you read about video girls twerking to LBJ in hell? Who else can pack microplastics, adultery, and overalls into the same poem, and make you (literally) cry along the way? No one, that's who. Sasha Debevec-McKenney is the real freaking deal.'
— Maggie Milner, author of *Couplets*

Fitzcarraldo Editions
8-12 Creekside
London, SE8 3DX
United Kingdom

Copyright © Sasha Debevec-McKenney, 2025
Originally published in Great Britain
by Fitzcarraldo Editions in 2025

The right of Sasha Debevec-McKenney to be identified as
the author of this work has been asserted in accordance with
Section 77 of the Copyright, Designs and Patents Act 1988.

ISBN 978-1-80427-187-2

Design by Ray O'Meara
Typeset in Fitzcarraldo
Printed and bound by Pureprint

All rights reserved. No part of this publication may be
reproduced, stored in a retrieval system or transmitted
in any form or by any means, electronic, mechanical,
photocopying, recording or otherwise, without prior
permission in writing from Fitzcarraldo Editions.

fitzcarraldoeditions.com

JOY IS MY MIDDLE NAME

SASHA DEBEVEC-MCKENNY

CONTENTS

CENTO FOR THE NIGHT I TRIED STAND-UP

☆

YOUR BRAIN IS NOT A PRISON!

SAMPLE OF MYSELF

THE STARS OF THE FAST & FURIOUS
FRANCHISE HAVE A CLAUSE IN THEIR
CONTRACTS THAT SAYS THEY CAN
NEVER LOSE A FIGHT

WHAT AM I AFRAID OF?

SESTINA WHERE EVERY END WORD
IS LYNDON JOHNSON

I DON'T HAVE A RACIST BONE IN MY BODY

ON DAYS I BELIEVE IN THE DEATH PENALTY

ON DAYS I DON'T BELIEVE IN
THE DEATH PENALTY

KAEPERNICK

BIOPIC IN WHICH I DON'T WANT
TO FALL IN LOVE BECAUSE I DON'T
WANT TO GAIN WEIGHT

PRAYER POEM

LIKE

LOOKING BACK

I BRING THE WART REMOVAL KIT WITH
ME TO THE JULY 4TH PARTY

I KNOW ALL ABOUT YOU, CAT MARNELL

I FEEL LIKE IF I'M NOT WRITING POLITICAL
POEMS I'M WASTING MY TIME SO I
MADE THIS CONTAINER FOR MYSELF
IN WHICH NOT TO BE POLITICAL

TUESDAY

I ALWAYS MAKE IT NICE (*REAL HOUSWIVES
OF NEW YORK* TAGLINES PANTOUM)

BERKSHIRES IN JULY

STAND-UP ROUTINE

JORDAN SAYS HE LOVES ME SO MUCH HE'LL
DELETE HIS INSTAGRAM FOR ME

WATCHING NATIONAL TREASURE
FOR THE FIRST TIME

ALONEDERLAND

I LIKE BEING CATCALLED WHILE I'M
SUICIDAL ON THE STREET IN WISCONSIN

HARTFORD HOSPITAL, NOVEMBER,
BARACK OBAMA IS PRESIDENT

JOHN BROWN'S BIRTHPLACE

DOING KARAOKE IN THE DESERT

FOR THE RECORD I REALLY WISH I TALKED
LESS BUT I LITERALLY CANNOT HELP IT

AT 33,

DOGSITTING POEM, CHICAGO,
JANUARY 2023

JOHNNY TEACHES ME HOW TO USE
A POWER DRILL IN REVERSE

ELECTION DAY,

ELEGY

TO NYC SASHA:

IT'S SO IDYLLIC HERE

I'M STARTING TO LIKE THIS
VERSION OF MYSELF, ACTUALLY,

NO FAP FOUND POEM

GRUDGE PERSON

I THOUGHT MY LIFE WAS OVER

JOY IS MY MIDDLE NAME

POEM AFTER MOVING AWAY

POEM FOR THE RACIST TOUR GUIDE
AT THE FRANKLIN PIERCE MANSE

WHEN I MET SHARON OLDS SHE TOLD ME TO
WRITE A POEM ABOUT LBJ'S PENIS

I WENT OUT TO SEE ALL THE
DOWNED TREES

IF YOU WANNA JUST SAY FUCK IT

☆

DEBTS, SOURCES, NOTES

CENTO FOR THE NIGHT I TRIED STAND-UP

Welcome to the place
where my jokes come from. Please
adjust your expectations, dear reader.
We've got a lot of shit to talk
about. I'm happy you're here.
I need you.

☆

I thought I'd start by sharing
my findings with you,
because knowledge shared
is knowledge halved. The universe began
with a big bang. But before that?
This is the question I asked
myself every night as a child.
Do mountains keep growing?
What's black and white and red all over?
Can you have a context-free word?
There's times in your childhood
you could really do with a drink.

☆

You don't know what to believe—
Taco Bell is selling chicken wings,
better believe something. Better
to have something to believe in.
I've seen UFOs split the sky like a sheet.
I believe that there is a God
and He hears our prayers
and is like, "Nah, fuck that."

☆

We're all guilty of something.
We don't even believe
in Heaven, but we're going.
How does this microphone
work? None of us know,

none of us know. None of us have ever known.
Look: some of this show is gonna be grim.
And I ask you: why does everything
have to be so good? I adore
a two-star experience. I think we all
have to ask a very important question
(and do try and be honest with yourselves
as you answer): *if you had an invisible hand,
what would you do with it?*

☆

I've been trying to trace
back my addictions.
What was my first addiction?
Whenever I investigate a smell,
the answer is always bad.
I can feel it in the room tonight.
I can feel it in the air,
I can taste it in the sky.

☆

Tipsy is the best thing you can be
in life; tipsy. There's four things you can be
in life: sober, tipsy, drunk, hungover.
Tipsy's the only one of four
where you don't cry.
It's warm and you're watching the sun
come up through the windshield.
And you see those stars up there,
and they're not even there,
it's just ... we're finally seeing
the light from those stars.

☆

People get the wrong idea about me.
They think I'm depressed or something.
I'm not depressed.
I bought a fourteen-dollar bar of soap once.
Three weeks ago, I put "nachos" in

as an Uber destination.
I was just recently named one of the top
five funniest people in America.
I suck at love. I love to party.
And I'm looking for a husband. Emotionally,
spiritually, genetically, historically,
I want to be a trophy wife. I may be dumb,
but I know right from wrong.
I do my judging silently.
Sometimes I go to the batting cage
just to play catch, as cute as I wanna be.
I'm jealous of people who get to meet me.
I have color headshots, 11 × 17;
I stand out in a pile.

☆

I can play archetypes or weather systems
but I can't play people. Orbiting
the earth, able to view the entire span
of human culture and existence and yet,
just because you have a thought
or a feeling, doesn't mean
it is always necessary
to express it. That's the real miracle.

☆

People tell you life is short. No,
it's not. Life is long. Especially if
you make the wrong decisions.
Somewhere over the rainbow
I bet life is just as exactly as hard
as it is on this side of the rainbow,
and on that side, you can't even see
a rainbow. There is nothing
you can do to us that we are not already doing
to ourselves. Should have warned you
earlier: some jokes are sad.

☆

Life is fucked up. Don't get me wrong,
there's brilliant bits, like when
you see someone you haven't seen
in a while, or get drunk unexpectedly,
or go for a cycle with the wind
behind you, or read a book
that's incredible, or you go
to an unbelievable show,
but very often when you get back
outside, you find that someone
set your bike on fire.

☆

Isn't there a part of you
that wants to die in the apocalypse?
All I'm saying is: if we all die
at the same time, it's like nobody died.
It's easy being dead. The hard thing
if you're a comedian
is to stay alive. I've monetized
a personality defect.
Do you guys like impressions?
Yeah? You do? Okay, good.
This is my impression
of a person doing impressions.

☆

I'm hiding nothing from you,
you guys are wonderful;
I'll tell you a personal story.
I went for a run the other day.
I accidentally swallowed a fly.
I had to google, "How many calories is a fly?"
I thought health equaled happiness
but that is not true. I know what you're thinking,
and the answer is: you can't put the genie back.

☆

I'm not really here
to make people accept their flaws.
This is just how I look.
Can I recommend that instead of war
to feel better about yourself,
perhaps, sit ups? Maybe a fruit cup?
Six to eight glasses of water a day?
I'm not telling you how to live,
I'm just recommending perhaps
a better way to feel better
about yourself. I want to make
a jigsaw puzzle that's 40,000 pieces
and when you finish
it says: GO OUTSIDE.

☆

There's no easy way of saying this:
we cannot, of course, harm
the president of the United States—
but it is not illegal to lead him
into a bramble, some uneven pavement,
rocky terrain. At its best,
America has never been
about facts. It's been about belief.
It's about looking at a fact
and saying, "No. No,
I don't think so,"
with all the confidence of a dog
running away from its own farts.

☆

I'm almost embarrassed to tell you
this: I'm supposed to want kids.
I don't know if I do.
I'm 30. I heard when you're a girl
and you're 30 you're just like,
I need a baby—but I don't want
to make anything with my body.

I don't need another reason to be hungry.
You ever go to throw a frisbee
and it's immediately sideways?
Can't have those moments back.

☆

A book walks into a bar
and sees a bookcase.
Everybody's trying to find
somebody. Let's form a club!
Who loves you?
Who do you go home to?
Aren't you sick of talking about it?

☆

Who here is in their twenties?
Leave your potential
alone. You'll screw it up,
don't look at it. Leave it there.
It's like your bank balance—
you always have less
than you think. In your mind
you think of potential as an unlocked door
within yourself; if you open the door
you'll see this wonderful palace,
gleaming marble floors, these endless
drapes, flamingos serving drinks
to elegant men and women arrayed
on chaise lounges exchanging witticisms,
somewhere between a wish
and an observation. But who
has time to enjoy a robe?

☆

I hate to end on a sad note.
What am I gonna leave you guys with?
"Wagon Wheel?"
We've had a good time.
We've laughed a lot.

We've learned a little.
You can spend
a decade on the wrong thing,
and before you realize it,
it's too late. If you're one
of the chosen few people
on earth that's lucky enough
to get your hands on a steak,
bite the shit out of it.
Thank you for knowing my name.
Goodnight.

"my metaphor my life"
— Wanda Coleman

"The yelp is not a sound of pain. It's a sound of joy."
— Lyndon Johnson

YOUR BRAIN IS NOT A PRISON!

A prison is the only place that's a prison.
Maybe your brain is a beehive—or, better:
an ants' nest? A spin class?
The sand stuck in an hourglass? Your brain is like
stop it. So you practice driving with your knees,
you get all the way out to the complex of Little League fields,
you get chicken fingers with four kinds of mustard—
spicy, whole-grain, Dijon, yellow—
you walk from field to field, you watch yourself
play every position, you circle each identical game,
each predictable outcome. On one field you catch.
On one field you pitch. You are center field. You are left.
Sometimes you have steady hands and French braids.
Sometimes you slide too hard into second on purpose.
It feels as good to get the bloody knee as it does to kick yourself in the shin.
You wait for the bottom of the ninth to lay your blanket out in the sun.
Admit it, Sasha, the sun helps. Today,
the red team hits the home run. Red floods every field.
A wasp lands on your thigh. You know this feeling.

SAMPLE OF MYSELF

"Most of us will sell pretty much anything pretty much all the time."
—*overheard*

Because this is Hell, I may or may not be wearing a visor,
and in this version of Hell, Hell is a Costco, and I am stuck in a booth.
My apron does not match my clothes, plus it cuts me in an unflattering
place at the hip, and I am setting out tiny paper cups,
but the cups refuse to be ordered sensibly in a three by four block—
the cup at the top left won't get in line with the other cups
but I can't even get mad because I know if I were a cup
I'd be *that* cup, the annoying cup, the cup that needed to prove itself
as better and different than the other cups, though I'm afraid
because I keep calling them cups you've started to visualize them
as regular-sized paper cups. But they're tiny. Somehow I fit.
Somehow, I'm fit to sample. Because this is Hell and everything is
obvious here and my hair looks bad and just when I think
it can't get worse, the Costco opens. I hear kids in the distance,
I can hear crying and spitting and farting and glass breaking.
They're getting closer. My cups aren't aligning. One of the kids yells,
"Mommy, I'm going to touch every single item for sale in this Costco!"
And the mom yells back, "I love you so much I'll pick you up
to reach the things on the highest shelves!" And the shelves are pretty high
in Costco, but this is less a Costco and more a Hell, time isn't real here,
and the kid touches every single item on sale in this Costco pretty quickly,
and I know I'm next, and I don't like being touched, but I don't get a choice
because I'm so for sale I'm on sale; I'm in every tiny cup.
I want it to stop but it won't. I try to leave my booth
but it's busy, the people in front of me
keep asking, "What is this?" "What is it for?" "Who is she?"
"How much does she cost?" "What does she do?" "Is that it?"
From the booths beside me I hear a more determined chant, a decisive
explanation of product: artisanal, organic, award-winning,
vegan, gluten-free, roll me round your mouth and make sure I hit
every point of the palate. I pitch my uses in anecdotal form—

great at bagging groceries! Tall but not too tall! Doesn't suffer fools!
Early riser! Will say the thing that everyone is thinking but is too afraid to
say! Buy me buy me buy me! Are they buying it?
I imagine a pile of myself by the register, abandoned
in the seconds before checkout.

THE STARS OF THE FAST & FURIOUS FRAN-CHISE HAVE A CLAUSE IN THEIR CONTRACTS THAT SAYS THEY CAN NEVER LOSE A FIGHT

All last fall I shouldn't have been driving.
I knew what a car could mean to a person and what a person
could mean to a person and I drove off the road instead.
I didn't really want to die.
Instead of saying I want to die
we should say I want to go to sleep.
We want pause. We want to hold ourselves in slow motion
having just driven off a cliff, to close our eyes and feel
the parachute pull us back, take a deep breath as the car flies
between two skyscrapers. Another spring, another sequel.
Give me Tyrese and Ludacris burning circles
into the moon, Michelle Rodriguez flipping
in zero gravity, Vin Diesel racing a spaceship to Mars
and winning. The franchise branches out.
The world introduces new villains.
I was not an Angry Drunk but fuck
I am an Angry Sober. Sobriety empties
all the hiding places. The world becomes a straight line.
You look Hate in the face like an old friend.
I never pictured getting the gang back together like this—
bare, alight, clamouring for a seat.
Paranoia keeps checking the airbag.
We pull up on Everyone Is Looking At Me
while he's in a meeting. I tap on the glass door and motion,
come with me. There is mounting sexual tension.
Disordered Eating has to tuck her daughter in for a nap.
She'll meet us at HQ, wearing something much tighter.
A Consuming Fear Of Death is out back in the garden.
He thought he had retired from this life.
I shake my head and he throws down his shovel.

WHAT AM I AFRAID OF?

The silence, the thoughts
that come with it, the sinking
suspicion that something more
is wrong with me than anyone
knows, including myself, including
the doctor who hooked me up
to the EKG machine and said
that though my heartbeat was irregular,
the irregularity was normal.
It was nothing to worry about.
The doctor told me there are two kinds
of people: unhealthy people who refuse
to get help, and healthy people
who always think they're dying.
Nobody's in-between. But I've met
so many kinds of people:
people who stretch before
they get out of bed, people
who walk through life unstretched,
people who think their body
is a house and people who don't
think of their bodies at all.
People who peel their carrots,
people who don't. People who
stand on the roof and let the wind
make them cry. People who are afraid
to cry. People who step on all the leaves
on the sidewalk, people who look
straight ahead. There are people
who aren't like me, they
don't know the names
of all the different apples.
Once when I was cashiering
a woman said to me, "Wow,

you really know your kale."
And once, at the butcher shop,
a man said to his dog, "That's
the nice lady who smells like meat."
I'm afraid I don't know
what kind of person I am.
I thought I would get a chance
to do my life over in all the ways
anyone could think of: dying
would be like changing the channel.
I hate that you can't hold on
to anything. I was washing an apple
and then I was coring it
and then it was cut—
and that was weeks ago, now.
It was a Honeycrisp, and it lived up
to its name.

SESTINA WHERE EVERY END WORD IS LYNDON JOHNSON

I am drinking water out of my dark green Lyndon Johnson
water bottle. I woke up this morning thinking about Lyndon Johnson.
I am only a third through a 3,000-page biography of Lyndon Johnson,
I saw a bird and it reminded me of Lyndon Johnson
because it had a nose like Lyndon Johnson's
and hopped from branch to branch like Lyndon Johnson.

My rhythm is Robert Caro's: wake up, Lyndon Johnson,
breathe, stretch, drink coffee, Lyndon Johnson,
walk down Central Park West, Lyndon Johnson,
dust off typewriter, Lyndon Johnson,
write about Lyndon Johnson, Lyndon Johnson,
die writing about Lyndon Johnson, Lyndon Johnson.

In August I flew to Austin, to the Lyndon Johnson
Presidential Library, and the Lyndon Johnson
Birthplace, and Grave, and to little Lyndon Johnson's
one-room schoolhouse, and to Lyndon Johnson's
Texas White House, and I camped out in that Lyndon Johnson
Hill Country and I swear all the stars were Lyndon Johnson.

If I try to imagine a world without Lyndon Johnson,
it's just the same world but I can tell Lyndon Johnson
is missing. And I think that's all Lyndon Johnson
ever wanted: for us to believe no one like Lyndon Johnson
exists, or existed. But he was barely Lyndon Johnson.
So who was Lyndon Johnson?

He tried hard to hide it but I looked at Lyndon Johnson
long enough to see Lyndon Johnson:
gangly-dark-haired-know-it-all Lyndon Johnson,
cheater-liar-refused-to-read-a-book Lyndon Johnson,
self-centered-fancy-dresser Lyndon Johnson,

three-packs-a-day-three-heart-attacks Lyndon Johnson,

I hate Lyndon Johnson until I love Lyndon Johnson,
I am eating Lyndon Johnson and sleeping Lyndon Johnson,
watching Lyndon Johnson watching Lyndon Johnson.

I DON'T HAVE A RACIST BONE IN MY BODY

My Ankle Break Support Group on Facebook was actually very supportive
When you get your cast off they say, "Oh look, another butterfly coming out of her shell!"

Six weeks leg elevated above heart, six weeks no walking, six weeks physical therapy
My father said, "In Civil War times they would have cut your leg off, Sasha."

The night I broke my ankle I say I wasn't that drunk but the further away I get from it the drunker I know I was

My favorite lie is *sorry, I have ice cream in my bag Ihavetogoitsmelting*

People keep saying I don't have a racist bone in my body
I've had a few racist bones in my body if you know what I mean

I said I was done with bartenders but Chris owned the bar
The break I blacked out but for months the pain made noise

CHRIS: We should do more than politic? xx
MALCOM X: If you pour too much cream in it, you won't even know you ever had coffee.

PLAYBOY MAGAZINE: Do black women throw themselves at you?
JOHN MAYER: I don't think I open myself to it. My dick is sort of like a white supremacist.

I jump at the sight of my own shadow—every single day I eat ice cream every day
My Podcast App reported over two weeks, thirty-seven hours spent listening to podcasts

My Ankle Break Support Group was infiltrated by men who wanted to paint our toenails red and rub themselves on our scars
Luckily I like my hair pulled

I never finished physical therapy
I sent my body away

Redbone is mostly now a porn word, meaning a light-skinned black woman you fuck from behind
Military surgeons in the Union Army performed over 30,000 amputations during the Civil War

ME: Tell that guy we don't say Black Manhattan anymore we say African American Manhattan, lol
CHRIS: You should hear what I call a Black Manhattan when you're not at the bar

You have to eat ice cream with your smallest spoon
When I'm in love I want to take a picture of everything

I am certain there was one time he filmed us without asking
I have two bars and four screws

Nobody will ever know how drunk I was
I wish I could find the tweet that was like mixed kids with white moms are born morally corrupt

33

Chris opened the curtains and said to the street, "Good morning, Frog Hollow! I am your gentrifier!"
"We don't know the numbers of Confederate amputations because the medical records went up in flames as the Davis administration fled Richmond."

I need attention I need attention I need attention I need attention I need attention I need attention I need attention I need attention
I need ice cream

People say they don't have a racist bone in their body
People say they don't have a racist bone in their body they do

In high school I got my bus driver fired for telling me he liked his women like his coffee light and weak
I will never feel sexier than leaning over the bar for Chris to give me a bump ne-ver

In Wisconsin I only had white friends and when I couldn't walk I only had white friends to take care of me Summer 2012 I took the detour off Jefferson Davis Highway to see where Stonewall Jackson's arm was buried

Is it easier to break racist bones are they weaker or stronger
You can touch my ankle if you want you can feel where the metal starts

On his fortieth birthday I blew him for forty minutes
I told a girl in cast and crutches one day you won't even remember you broke it you'll just use your legs

Stonewall's men thought his body would survive without the arm but it didn't
White girls carrying my breve lattes from counter to table, moving my chair from the patio to shower, around my couch in a circle below me

You've heard of standing up for what's right but what about lying down with your face in the mattress and your ass up for free drugs
If you have health insurance, it really is worth the attention, breaking a bone

I learned to love my body by sending nudes
Everything I've done to get better, all my self-improvement, I did it for a man

It is nice to throw the ice cream lid away immediately, knowing you will never close the container
I don't think the body lets us remember physical pain, said the girl

ON DAYS I BELIEVE IN THE DEATH PENALTY

After Birmingham, non-violence
wasn't holding down its side of the scale.
I guess to learn not to hate
you have to learn to hate, first.
In polite conversation at an otherwise
empty bar, a man told me
he was proud his family fought
for the Confederacy, and I said I wish
your whole bloodline had ended there:
thin and shoeless on a battlefield,
neck blown open. I got kicked out
of the bar. Tonight, in Bushwick,
in line at a taco truck pop-up,
in the middle of an art gallery,
I thought to myself, this wouldn't be the worst place
for a bomb to go off.

AND ON DAYS I DO NOT BELIEVE IN THE DEATH PENALTY,

I still live on the same earth as Dylann Roof,
where being an organ donor feels like tempting fate,
a red mark on my driver's license giving away my secret:
I have a heart in my body and you can take it
out of my body if you want!
RFK said, *a white man killed my brother, too,*
then never talked about it in public again.
It probably isn't true but at the end of the war
somewhere South, Lincoln asked,
where is the oldest slave in this town?
And then led him to a pile of Confederate money
and handed him a match.

KAEPERNICK

My mother is uncomfortable with my top.
She doesn't think my boobs should be
out like this. She adjusts the TV antenna and says,
"Isn't the TV working better now?" I don't want
to watch football. I am trying to learn to do my makeup.
My mother never taught me. Should I say at this point
that my mother is white? I used to watch Pantene commercials
and think my hair could look like that if I used enough
of her product. She has one of those white-mom
haircuts now. It is thinning. She needs more volume.
She needs me to tell her I know I'm white too.
Like I think about anything else. The football players
are kneeling because, I say, anyone could kill
your black son. He's white, too, she says—and you
could use a little more eyeliner. She wonders
why I don't want her to help me pick out foundation.
The football players stand up. Then they play football.

BIOPIC IN WHICH

I am probably born in a storm,
a savior, a raging metaphor,
signifying something
for my mother, though
I'm not sure what. In childhood:
an experience that shows I'm different
from the other children. Naturally,
I grow too tall, too fast.
My first word is a full sentence
and my parents are convinced
I'm special. Maybe I am special.
Either way, I have to leave. Promise
I won't change. Cue montage:
sweat, blood, blah, blah, blah,
a little light trauma, some semi-violence,
nothing that will upset the audience
of course: front teeth knocked out
with a softball, a beloved aunt's death,
a problematic college boyfriend,
some regular microaggressions,
and smash cut: I am swept up in
success: I am wanted, swarmed,
I duck into a dark car, I have no
alone time but, oh, I feel so
alone. Then: more men.
Alcohol, some drugs.
A smoky back room, a zoom
in on my face as I experience an altered
reality for the first time. How much
do I love it? There aren't words.
But the much-more-attractive-than-me-
actor who is playing me does her best
to show it on her face.
People are worried about her

but don't know how to tell her,
etcetera, etcetera. However bad
they show it on screen, know
it was ten times worse to feel.
Every indulgence makes her
wonder more and more,
who have I become?
You know. It doesn't matter
who loves me, there isn't
a moral or a lesson. I luxuriate
in my expansive collection
of robes. I long to fake
my own death. Time passes.
My mother takes me back.
A few wrinkles painted gently
on the soon-to-be-Oscar-winning-actor's
forehead, she sits in a window and watches
a storm approach—a storm not unlike the storm
that rolled into town the night
I was born. I welcome the storm,
scream, beat my fists against
the glass. The filmmaker shuffles
his deck of flashbacks. My body
slumps against the window.
You can see, in letting go, I seem
to have finally found some peace.

I DON'T WANT TO FALL IN LOVE BECAUSE
I DON'T WANT TO GAIN WEIGHT

but I drank 800 calories of bourbon with him last night
and this morning I was so hungover I would have let myself have it,
a bagel, but I couldn't move, dumb struck with my hands down my
pants until I had to go to work. No time. I talk myself back
into eating the overnight oats in the fridge. Flax seeds.
Unsweetened almond milk. Once something goes into your body
it's in your body for good. Your thighs, butt, stomach.
Last week walking in the park he asked, what kind of food do you like?
I said healthy, he said I've been craving wings.
Me too, but I get mine unsauced. He tells me the truth
about his girlfriend. He adds more and more to the scale.
I shouldn't have put cream in my coffee this morning. Two servings.
One for me and one for the version of me that lets herself fall in love.
She isn't scared to gain anything. To tell him to keep feeding me
like before I lost weight; I'm thinking about seconds
and thirds with all of this still on my plate. It's like dipping bacon
into maple syrup. It's egg yolk dripping down the hand. It's the hand
up my shirt. Last night the bartender told us we needed to get a room
and that was all I wanted: to be in a room with him.
I told her well actually we can't, we're having an affair,
there isn't a room we can go to. This is our room. I made it for us.

PRAYER POEM

It was Sunday and the Packers were losing. I started praying. I readied my offer to God. I was praying for the Packers to win. Dear God, I said, if you let the Packers win, I'll never drink again. Then I remembered my beer, half-finished and waiting for me. Never mind, God, I said. Never mind. I'll think of something else. I looked around the room. There was, in the room, a man I did not intend on giving up on quite yet, a TV I would not watch less of, a floor I wouldn't sweep more. The Packers lost. For what must have been the first time in my life, I couldn't think of anything I was willing to give up or change about myself. I had prayed before to wake up different. I had begged God to change many things about my life, like who my parents were, or for a bead door to my bedroom, or to make me married to my favorite baseball player. I had even changed myself many times, with no one's help. I changed myself, for instance, into a person who hikes. I hiked to the top of a hill in Indian Lake Park where in 1857 a man built a tiny blue chapel—he promised God he'd build a chapel if his family survived the diphtheria epidemic—the snow on the path to the chapel had iced over, so I slid my way up the hill, falling every few feet to find myself face to face with some animal's blood, spilled into the snow. The blood continued up the entirety of the trail. I reminded myself that animals killed each other all the time. I needed new boots. My Timberlands were six years old and had holes—I prayed to God for new Timberlands. I prayed for warmer feet, I prayed to stop falling. The chapel was surrounded by a black fence. The chapel was about the size of my kitchen. Inside, there were multiple pictures of Mary. In the chapel, beneath two Marys, on top of the hill, there was a prayer book full of prayers. Moms had written down prayers for their kids who couldn't write yet. Kids prayed for the family dog, who did not know prayers existed. Aunts and uncles were in the hospital, maybe God had time to help? Reading other people's prayers felt dirty, but I didn't stop. I rationalized. I was certain my reading them only made them stronger.

LIKE

As I led the man through
the crowded restaurant
and to his table at the back
he said, "You sure are packing
us in here like on slave ships,"
when he could have said
anything else: packing us in here
like daisies into a grocery-store
bouquet, packed together
like the pages of a wet book,
like A-listers in a Wes Anderson movie,
like hemorrhoid cream in an unopened tube,
like pennies in a pickle jar,
like forty to fifty exuberant,
rural children in an underfunded
classroom, like a family of polar bears
crowded together on a floating sheet of ice—
he could have said, even,
like your ass in those jeans.

Blood in a syringe, silver compact
vehicles on the Beltline at rush hour,
Styrofoam tight in its cardboard box.
Yes, I was packing him in there,
like textured ground-beef material
into a Taco Bell Grilled Stuft Burrito,
like Amish girls in the back of a white van
on the way to Walmart. Like bone regrowing
inside a plaster cast. Like the flames
in a fire, like the fingers in my fist.

LOOKING BACK

shit was fucked
up. We were broker
than we thought, living
off tips, committing
check fraud, lending
each other cat food,
bumming cigarettes
back and forth,
making ourselves
sick, saying yes
too much, losing condoms
inside us, breaking bones
that would never totally
heal, stealing weed, shooting
Tullamore Dew, demanding
the bartender play
"Torn." We weren't safe
on the bike path,
there should have been
more light.

I BRING THE WART REMOVAL KIT
WITH ME TO THE JULY 4TH PARTY

because I never read instructions right, and to freeze something off
my body seems like too much for me, who is not a doctor,
to do alone, though I have done my research: warts grow
on compromised skin, a white man tattooed FEAR ITSELF
on my wrist ten years ago, and I shouldn't have let him
get that close to me in the first place—I should have known
a wart would grow there eventually, slowly at first,
and then by this mid-summer a giant O where the E
in FEAR used to be, a white orb, and I should have known not
to mark myself as so American, even though my first memory
is standing below a WWII display at the FDR museum
holding my white mother's hand and feeling fear for the first time,
even though every morning I ate only off the presidents placemat
and sloppily, so sometimes the sugared cereal lines crossed out
their faces, and I'm American too: I bought the most expensive
wart removal kit they had at Target and I'll end up throwing it away—
that's how American I am, I don't care what I waste, I named
all my dolls Eleanor Roosevelt, even the black Barbies—
the excuses are how the wart got this bad in the first place.

I KNOW ALL ABOUT YOU, CAT MARNELL
found poem from *How to Murder Your Life*

Being clean felt great in Connecticut. But back in Manhattan,
not being on stimulants just felt... wrong. My energy didn't match the
city's. I stared grimly at a pile of arugula, the most boring salad in the
world. I sat at a fancy table and tried to will a plate of gnocchi to turn
into cocaine. Glamour. G-L-A-M-O-U-R! What more could I want?
The white walls matched the white notes in the fragrance; the sleek,
minimalist white bottle. There were white candles, white napkins, white
orchids at every table. Even the marketing people were white. I was *very*
privileged, and *very* cold. I was a senior at Sleeping Pill College, Tanning
Bed University. I had *Vanity Fair* for brains. *Best Drugstore Mascara?*
Maybelline Great Lash. Check. *Best Department Store Mascara? Lancôme*
Définicils. Check. *Best Department Store Fragrance? Britney Spears Curious.*
Check. *Adderall.* Check! October was flat, and darker. I'd flunked out of
girl-world. I smelled like Mustela vanilla, Kiehl's coriander lotion, and
marijuana. The only guys I let into the bubble... well. Recluses get weak,
as Jenny Holzer said. And forget intimacy. Speed was like magic! Lonely
magic. Lonelier and lonelier. I didn't know how to cook, and I didn't know
how to fall asleep. "Slow DOWN!" I'd scream, but he never did. I knew the
man outside was bad, but I buzzed the bad man up. I preferred Vyvanse to
boyfriends. "No one can make you feel anything you don't want to feel,"
my mother told me once; a delusion. By January, I was *ridin' for a fall*.
Days were for writing. Nights I never said no. "I am VERY healthy and
normal!" I wrote. *Rolling Stone* called me Hot Bukowski. I was trying to
pass for human in a world where women didn't even have split ends. I was
not afraid of making eye contact. I went through crazy phases.
I can't handle this, I thought, immediately, *without Adderall*. My addiction
finished the thought for me. My mostly companion. Like two boxers in
a ring for years. My ambition was bloodied, bruised, and—finally, now—
defeated. *Ding ding ding.* Addiction won. That is supposed to be a bell. I
got out of the bath again. I exhaled—rehab was just a place where a party
girl could recharge her batteries, a building that Mariah Carey rented
for herself after she went on *TRL* and pushed that ice-cream cart around
without any pants on—what was I going to wear? I stood in my closet,

despairing. Silver Hill really should make a candle. There was this enormous black poodle that got walked around sometimes. We all got to pet it, but I've never truly connected with a poodle. Have you? The lesson: it's really hard to get sober in your twenties! Slather some sixty-nine-dollar Organic Pharmacy Rose Balm on your open wounds, then get right back to work. I'd been washing my hair sitting down in the bathtub. I had a lot of hair and I didn't rinse very well. Zero exercise, triple amphetamines: your legs absolutely start to look like arms. I slept through March. Ecstasy and OxyContin decidedly do *not* mix; I mixed them anyway. I'd been collaging since I moved in. I woke at strange hours: *HELP*, Jack Pierson scratched out on one drawing of a mascara wand. *LIFE IS A KILLER*, it read over a photo of William S. Burroughs. *INSANE!* the Britney-on-a-gurney *Star* cover read. *WAS IT MURDER?* was the headline of the Anna Nicole Smith *New York Post* front page. This toxicity comforted me. It made me feel less alone. But I wasn't there—inside my body. The bouts of shame came and went every hour. *No Signal.* The words on the blue screen bounced around. *No Signal. No Signal. No Signal.* I pocketed a button that read: I <3 TERROR. I walked out onto the street and put my headphones on. *It's Britney, bitch.* It was a gorgeous early evening. I saw it all in my dumb mind. Over time, I'd learn to turn the volume down on SHAME FM, but I could never totally shut it off.

I FEEL LIKE IF I'M NOT WRITING POLITICAL POEMS I'M WASTING MY TIME SO I MADE THIS CONTAINER FOR MYSELF IN WHICH NOT TO BE POLITICAL

The first thing I thought this morning was that Mayonnaise would be a good name for a dog. I could scream *Mayonnaise! Mayonnaise, Mayonnaise!* into the dark of my backyard.

Whenever anybody in my life travels anywhere the only thing I ask them is what was the best thing you ate? Tobias keeps a clog keychain on his keys that reminds him of French fries he ate in Amsterdam.

On Saturday he dumped a bag of individually wrapped chocolates onto my bed and not thinking we lay down and crushed all ten pieces. Repeatedly. Then we shared a melted, flat Ferrero Rocher.

Outside my apartment someone set a tin of breadcrumbs and rocks, the breadcrumbs to eat and the rocks to hold down the tin.

Windsor, Connecticut was one of a handful of towns in the country where, in the 2000 Census, median income for black households was larger than for white households and I was a girl.

It rained and I remembered cutting earthworms in half with the plastic shovel in the Montessori sandbox.

I broke my arm skipping monkey bars on that playground. I was never a girl who shared.

I was wearing the knit sweater with the purple whales and I was warm. A woman screamed: *Your hair! Your sweater! A texture paradise!*

Someone told me they're calling the other Sasha at work White Sasha.

My fingers pruned the second I stepped in the shower and it scared me. All my other fears are political. I was never a girl.

Colleen called, *I'm in town, my dad had the best possible heart attack.* He walked over to the trainer, sat down and said I'm having a heart attack.

The men working at the barber shop turned up the light so I could read while I waited for the hair braider.

When I'm getting my hair braided, I get to miss my grandmother and be in physical pain at the same time.

My sister visited Tuesday because she had Lincoln's birthday off. *Did he even do anything other than get shot?*

I was so proud of myself I said *not really!* I tossed my scarf over my shoulder and kept walking.

TUESDAY

our ATM broke so bad
they took it away
and brought us a new one.
The man with the dolly
rolling it out chuckled
in defeat. He didn't want
to give us more work but
admittedly this was
an opportunity
to sweep somewhere
that never got swept.
I took it. A full bottle
of sanitizer was back there,
the Yellow Pages, an entire
restaurant's worth of dirt, some of
the white powder we sprinkled
around the kitchen
to stop the cockroaches
migrating over
from the place next door
(it didn't matter, in the end,
the health inspector had said
through her crisp blue mask—
there were cockroaches
in every restaurant
on Willy Street). The ATM
man—and other men
who come to restaurants
to do maintenance on complicated
machines like ATMs
or dishwashers, are always
so hot, they squat
a lot and show up
exclusively to fix your problems—

after placing and plugging
in the new ATM then
running three separate,
successful transactions,
showed me the tiny hole
beneath the ATM's card slot:
"You ever get a card stuck
in there, you get a pushpin,
you stick it in the hole,
the card'll unstick,
you'll be a hero." Then
the restaurant got
so busy so fast I couldn't
finish this poem and
give it the nice ending
it deserved. It filled up
so all of a sudden, as if
all the couples in the
neighborhood had woken
to the same alarm,
the same hungers—and
when the ATM man
almost hit a loved-up
hippie in her heel
with his empty dolly
on the way out,
she didn't care,
because she had just come
from having sex
and now she was going
to have French toast,
with chocolate chips,
and whipped cream.

I ALWAYS MAKE IT NICE (*REAL HOUSEWIVES OF NEW YORK* TAGLINES PANTOUM)

I'm living the American dream one mistake at a time.
I'm not afraid to say what everyone else is thinking.
I never feel guilty about being privileged.
The only thing I'll settle for is more.

I'm not afraid to say what everyone else is thinking.
If you can't handle the truth, you can't handle me.
The only thing I'll settle for is more.
Not everything I say is clear, but it's always clear what I'm saying.

If you can't handle the truth, you can't handle me.
I'm living the American dream one mistake at a time.
Not everything I say is clear, but it's always clear what I'm saying.
I never feel guilty about being privileged.

BERKSHIRES IN JULY

The road sign said IGNORE GPS.
The train full of recyclables passed
underneath me. The furniture store
was not simply going out of business,
but selling down to its bare walls.
In an attempt to aid digestion,
I was consciously chewing longer.
I was on vacation, lax about recycling.
The movie theater was only
a ten-minute walk, so I went five times.
I kept losing cell phone service, forcing
my therapist to repeat, "Do you hear me?
Do you hear me? Do you hear me now?"
Caught in a thunderstorm, I felt hot
and forgiven. In old journals,
I want the same things
I want now. Yoga, walk,
don't waste time, don't eat carbs.
On top of the highest peak
in Massachusetts, I peed
into a Dunkin Donuts cup.
Since last week, when the monarch
butterfly was declared endangered,
I've seen four of them.

STAND-UP ROUTINE

So I was watching *Babe* last night, you know,
the movie where the pig herds sheep?
And I can't stop thinking about the people
in the crowd at the sheep herding competition,
who saw the pig herd sheep—I mean, go
rewatch the movie, you can see some of these extras
giving the performance of a lifetime, their lives change
on their faces—they've just seen something truly, truly
remarkable. Like, imagine you've been going
to sheep herding competitions your whole life;
you grew up doing it, your father did it, his father.
And now you want your grandson to herd sheep,
it's only right and natural, and so one Sunday,
you take him to lunch at your favorite diner,
and you tell your favorite waitress you don't need
another refill, and then the two of you drive out
to the sheep herding competition, and you sit smugly
on the benches, knowing exactly what to expect.
And then the pig comes out and herds the sheep.
It's almost as if—and you feel crazy for thinking this—
the pig is actually *talking* to the sheep? Your face
opens. Your world changes. What sporting event
could ever top this? One weekend your grandson invites you
to his football game, he never got into herding sheep
after all, and that's fine, because you love him,
and he scores the final goal, and the team lifts him up
on their shoulders, and the whole time you're thinking,
well, this isn't as impressive as when I saw that pig herd sheep.
It's merely *the truth*! You're proud of your grandson,
he's got a scholarship for the fall, but it objectively
isn't as impressive. Nothing is. You used to love
the bacon and tomato sandwich at that diner:
the bacon was thick, the black pepper was freshly ground,
salt flakes fat. But it's not as good as when you saw

the pig herd sheep. *I don't think they use
freshly ground pepper anymore,* you say,
to your grandson, *I mean, the sandwich is still g
ood but it isn't—as good as the time we saw the pig,*
he finishes. He makes eye contact with the waitress.
Talking about that pig again, Gary? she asks,
dropping the check. You pay the check. You kiss
your grandson on his cheek. He leaves for school
tomorrow. You promise yourself you will relearn
how to be impressed by your life. You will try
to see something every day that *could, possibly*
be better than seeing the pig herd sheep.
You go to the grocery store. You buy white bread,
name brand mayonnaise, thick cut bacon.
You thank God it is tomato season. You remake
the sandwich from the diner, exactly the way you like it.
It isn't even hard. The sandwich is perfect.
You're impressed by yourself, and by your innate
ability to make a punchline of the world
right back. You laugh out loud into your empty kitchen.

JORDAN SAYS HE LOVES ME SO MUCH
HE'LL DELETE HIS INSTAGRAM FOR ME

After everything, I still have to explain this to him:
you can't turn me into someone who sees a rock as a rock.
If I am stranded on an island something is going to happen
on this island that I am meant to see. If I am starving
I'm supposed to report back on how it feels to starve. I belong
on this beach. Using only my mind, I can turn a rock
into a roasted chicken. Hunger is a feeling.
A feeling is a strength. Strength a type of magic.

It's too late for small gestures, Jordan. God already invented
man. Men invented last names. Men were not worthy
of last names, so they shared them with women.
The men and women give last names to their children.
The children try to do enough to earn them.
If they love the name enough they practice it.
Sometimes they practice so much we write their last names
on the backs of our shirts. The last name becomes an outline
of the body, jumping. The body becomes a factory. We sing its songs.
We fill stadiums with boys, all wearing the same sneakers,
shouting, "Jumpman, Jumpman, Jumpman, Jumpman" which to me
is now another song about Jordans I can't listen to anymore.

One time I offered to come over and watch TV with a heartbroken friend
and she said, "Don't judge me for this, but I can't watch TV right now.
Andrew and I used to watch TV together." I'll set goals to distract myself
like, Go To Every Goodwill In The State Of Connecticut.
I'll find a map of Operation Iraqi Freedom that is actually
a scarf, wash it by hand, wait for it to dry, wrap my hair
up for the night and see Jordan across my forehead. Of course
you're a country. I will Go To Every Goodwill In Connecticut.
I will walk down the kitchen aisle to turn each mug and read,
"World's Best Jordan!" or "I'm Not Jordan Until I Drink My Coffee!"

Don't judge me for this, but at Goodwill when a woman asks me
if I speak Spanish, if I can translate the faded recipe on the soup bowl
in her hands, I say, "No, No. I speak Jordan. It says if you add
Jordan to Jordan and wait long enough they will combine
to make Jordan. "Haven't you heard all the songs?" She's like,
"Do you speak Spanish or not?" She hands me the bowl
and I'm like, "This isn't mine." But then the bowl turns into a rock.
She grows a beard. She's Jordan. Jordan says, "It was all a trick.
Let's go back inside."

WATCHING *NATIONAL TREASURE* FOR THE FIRST TIME

And of course I asked myself, could I...steal the Declaration
of Independence?
No. Obviously. I just had a crying fit after failing to French braid my
hair.
Then I checked the Facebook of the wife of the Married Guy I was in
love with in 2015
to make sure their baby was still ugly. It was. And about halfway
through the movie
I passed out drunk. It was 4.30 p.m. What was it the Founding Fathers
said?
"If there's something wrong, those who have the ability to take action
have the responsibility
to take action?"—or was that Nicolas Cage in *National Treasure*? My
Married Guy
was a painter. He showed me a painting of him and his wife as
American Gothic.

Their faces were painted blue to signify oxygen deprivation. He ripped
the painting in half
and said, "I will never have children with her." That line was on every
list I found later,
when I googled, "lies married men tell you." I knew that *American
Gothic* was a painting
of a father and a daughter, not a painting of a husband and a wife, but I
knew that most men
did not like when I lectured them on the value of historical accuracy. I
wanted to believe
in hidden treasure, too, so I didn't correct him.

*ALONE*DERLAND

It snowed again last night, which meant this morning
I could track my neighbor's dog pissing his way across my backyard
and over to the water, where I could see my own deflated tracks
from yesterday, I tried to walk on the lake but then I heard
a crack. I stepped in my own footprints on the way back.
Four months ago, I was out here burning my unread newspapers
strip by strip, toasting marshmallows perfectly gold then throwing
them into the dark water. Now my hammock straps were frozen
to the tree. Last year I didn't think it was so special to be sharing
something as simple as a couch. There was even someone
I shared a couch with often, and we held our breath together
to see who could last longest. I lost. This Christmas he sent me
a box full of pine cones and a fraying vintage globe, I held it in my
hand. I was supposed to paint the pine cones with peanut butter
and roll them in seeds. This way, I would make friends with the birds.
Some birds were already stopping on the little deck off my kitchen.
I could see the lines of their feet in the snow, too.
I never noticed animals like this
until I started a survivalist show on the HISTORY Channel
where ten contestants film themselves alone in the Arctic.
They have no choice but to notice the animals.
They build log cabins out there and make chimneys from clay.
They suck out squirrel guts and slice up porcupine livers.
They cry into the camera as bears move past camp;
one woman chanted, "I know I will be safe, I know I will be safe."
She hadn't had a bowel movement in ten days.
The graphic across the television read: *constipation*
is one of the most life-threatening symptoms of starvation.
And that's when I realized I had been starving myself
for most of 2018. And I remembered being so lightheaded
on a walk down Bedford I almost passed out. I moved
myself slowly through the CVs checkout line
with a dark chocolate KitKat bar, which I ate while leaning in the sun.
For a real survivalist, fat is the most important thing you can have,

so they thank the lake for its trout, they thank the sap,
they thank the rabbit after twisting its neck,
they thank the moose for its tongue. They get so lonely.
They make playing cards out of birch bark. They would kill
for a book. I clicked the *on* switch on my new clear electric kettle.
I already had a kettle on my stovetop, but it wasn't fast enough.
There was nothing to be on time to, and nobody waiting for me,
but I wanted to see the water while it boiled, glowing blue.
Outside, the lake was freezing. I didn't want to freeze with it.

I LIKE BEING CATCALLED
WHEN I'M SUICIDAL

so I put on my good jeans and go for a walk.
Because I like hearing my body parts listed.
Because the birdsong could be for anybody.
Because I need to be told I am alive
by someone who could not possibly
know the awful things I've done,
because when I saw the spilled ice cubes
on the sidewalk I thought
in any other season
you would have melted
then I stepped on them.
Because nobody else noticed
I got up off my floor
and left my apartment building
except the man across the bar
who grabbed my jaw and said,
"You know how good you look,"
squeezed harder and said,
"You're so fucking stuck up!"
Because when a man sees me
from the front and the back and still
shouts he wants to marry me, I think maybe,
maybe with him I could have a life.

ON THE STREET IN WISCONSIN

The door to the dive bar opened
and a black woman walked out.
I could smell summer in there behind her—
rank and hot and close and shoulders—
outside it was already September, almost next year—
I love your hair, she mouthed, and it ran through me like beer
through a dirty tap line and into a freshly polished glass.

HARTFORD HOSPITAL, NOVEMBER, BARACK OBAMA IS PRESIDENT

My grandmother rarely
called us by our real names
but you knew when she meant you.
I was the youngest girl
so I had the most names. Yes
her sentences had always
trailed off into little mysteries to me
but when she was dying

and the doctor asked her
what month it was
she said November
and I thought oh, good,
so she isn't dying
she knows it's November.
But she didn't know the year.
And she didn't know the President.
The doctor left. It was just me,
my brother and my grandmother

and the CNN anchor saying
JFK was killed fifty years ago
this month,
my grandmother saying
do they know who shot him yet,
my brother saying no,
and death pulling its drawstring,
closing us all inside.

JOHN BROWN'S BIRTHPLACE

is an hour away from mine. I never knew I never
knew all the history here. At the Historical Society
they told me there was no information on the black solider
from my hometown who fought in the Civil War.
"That's too late for us!" So I did it myself.
That summer I looked at every gravestone
in Windsor, Connecticut. I found him in the cemetery
behind the church where I did Girl Scouts. I was not
the only black Girl Scout, I was never the only black girl
on my basketball team. My dad was never not my coach.
What radicalized me? My father's questions
in my childhood: "Why were there were no black people
in that commercial, Sasha? Is that really the cereal you want?"
"Why is the black Spice Girl named Scary Spice? What about her
is scary?" "Do you think there's a McKenney tribe in Africa?"
"Why aren't you reading August Wilson in your playwrighting class?"
The next day I went into my playwrighting class and asked
my teacher why. We read *Fences* two weeks later.
My Granny was only 18 when she had my father and decided to leave
Virginia, but in a book they'd call that the Great Migration.
She was supposed to get off the train in New York City
but it scared her too much. It was too loud. So we grew up
in Connecticut instead. Sometimes history is as simple as that.

DOING KARAOKE IN THE DESERT

Merging onto the highway that morning it said TAKE TURNS!
We had planned to have a No Kill day—all vegetables—
and then we ran over a lizard. And at that point
you may as well eat a burger. I let myself get drunk
because I'm on vacation. And I don't allow myself
to mourn the time I will lose. Nobody will remember me
but at a karaoke bar that's a good thing.
"Don't be nervous," says the other guy picking a song,
"This is all a shameless train wreck."

I'm learning. I always thought Joshua Tree was one big tree
where people held hands and found themselves.
But Joshua Tree is thousands of trees, and this is the only place
this kind of tree survives. Every creature in the desert takes
from the Joshua tree until the trees crumble into the earth.
When they grow, they grow two inches per year.
The more I see of my country, the more I realize
how much of it does not look like where I grew up.
In another life I might have seen a forest and thought,
this is what the desert would look like wet.

I'm in the desert. The animals survive by burying
themselves and burying their water.
I hate to be enjoying the same earth as the white man
leaning against his Mustang pulling cactus quills out of his arm
outside the cactus garden but what else can you do
when you realize at the end of the world
it will be even hotter than this?
And you will be thirsty. And you see
every one of your selves dying out.
It doesn't matter that I can't sing. I sing anyway.

FOR THE RECORD I REALLY WISH I TALKED LESS BUT I LITERALLY CANNOT HELP IT
found poem from my tweets, 2009–2021

They say a watched pot never boils but they're lying because I am literally watching one come to a boil right now. It took me two hours to wake up—I literally had to drink a Diet Coke in bed. I literally posted a pic on Instagram begging for validation and people gave it to me. I literally dreamed about chocolate. I literally paused the "Yoga to Calm Your Nerves" video. I PMS-ed for literally a month and a half. I literally spent fifteen minutes spilling beans, then cleaning them up, then spilling them again. I am literally writing a letter I will never send to somebody who will never love me the way I want to be loved. We are literally insignificant, literally burnt. I am literally sweating gin today, and I literally need pink camouflage loungewear right now. I have literally never been so awake in my life. I literally broke the CD I listened to it so much! I am literally sitting on a swing in the middle of a field of snow, I literally cry about a different dead black person every single day, literally tell me what to feel and I'll feel it— I literally took the train into the city at 6 a.m., I literally never shut the fuck up. My backyard is literally a lake. I literally need a hug. I literally got a master's degree and felt nothing. I literally don't know what I'm doing but I'm trying my hardest. Literally how do you wear sandals? Literally what are you supposed to say when someone says you smell good? Literally what is a map? I literally do not understand jewelry. And is there anything in the world more painful than literally having normal emotions? I literally think everything is about me and especially the weather for some reason. I literally got my period in the middle of getting a tattoo and the tattoo was of crying eyes. I literally had the worst twenty-four hours. I am literally so grateful every time I laugh. I literally love you. I literally need more details. I am literally setting a timer for half an hour. I literally shed a single tear. My jaw literally dropped.

AT 33,

I have no problems
touching a stranger's
underwear in the laundromat.
I don't idle, I recycle,
I always dig the caramel
ribbon out of the pint
of ice cream. I know
what's coming for me
which is why I try not to judge
my friends for their small
bladders. Once a week
someone stops me
on the street to say, "You're so pretty!"
It's not enough. I'm only willing
to drive eight miles over
the speed limit. I get a little lonely
when I pull my car into the driveway
and see my car's not there.
My biggest ick is littering.
I've only slept with one girl;
she looked exactly like me.
My body is an optical illusion.
My hometown was founded
in 1633. I still want a baby.
My relationship with alcohol
is no more complicated
than my relationship with any other
substance in the universe.
I could go find someone
to sleep with at the bar, but
I already have that T-shirt.
The man who helped me move
my dresser out of the estate sale
said he could tell by my sweat

that my organs were working correctly.
I don't want to date
anyone whose family came over
on the *Mayflower* again. On Sundays,
I purchase an expensive decaf latte
and go on a three-hour walk. I want
to be taken care of and I need
to be kissed. I did a foot peel
and peeled all the dead skin
off my feet. So if we meet,
my feet will feel so smooth
and so brand new.

DOGSITTING POEM, CHICAGO, JANUARY 2023
for Pico

Sometimes you have to get out of town to talk to your friends in town, you know? Zakk called while I was walking my friend's dog, in Chicago, the first week of January. He's going to name his son Theodore Jeffrey. Ted, Theo, Teddy, TJ— "Never TJ. I don't know him yet, but I know he's not TJ." I held the phone away from my face, like a newborn, in awe of the future's existence. The whole week I dogsat, I walked around thinking, "I can't wait to meet TJ," knowing he'd always be TJ to me; that's how I am. I must have looked so dumb, smiling like that. All over Chicago, scooping shit. But I was so happy. The dogsitting apartment had perfect writing lighting, high ceilings, an extra bedroom, in-fridge water.

By the third day of dogsitting, the dog's eyes had softened, and were softening me, my shoulders lowered visibly and it didn't even occur to me to smoke weed until past five. The cleanse was working. Sometimes you just have to get out of town. Especially if in your town, in Wisconsin, at that very moment, a local Native American activist was being outed as a white woman born Katie. She was tanning like two times a week, killing herself from the inside and the outside, taking years off everyone's lives—but honestly, the dog I was sitting was so beautiful, like star-of-stage-and-screen, luxurious-black-coat, Cary-Grant-love-interest beautiful, I physically couldn't, in her presence, think about the capacity white women have to do evil.

It was so nice to walk beside someone whose pace I had to keep up with, not the other other way around. Usually, when I walk, I have a hard time telling whether people are walking toward me or away from me. In the city it felt easy; everyone on every sidewalk, we were all going the right way. None of us would have to turn around because we forgot our breakfast on the counter.

The weather was perfect and I dressed perfectly for it. The pillows lacked the structure I liked but my dreams had sturdy narratives: I was taking the train to Memphis, to Graceland, and I was willing to admit I was a black person who loved Elvis. I was only human. The dogsitting instructions told me where all the best tacos in the area were. We were in a Mexican American neighborhood on the west side. Handmade tortillas were a foregone conclusion. And still, I didn't crave tacos. And it was okay. I ordered pickle pizza instead, extra pickles.

Yoga would balance out the pickle pizza, and yoga had to balance out losing my brand-new gloves on the walk home with the pickle pizza. The pizza was so salty, but I had a salt tooth. Salt is my favorite flavor. Someone had graffitied GENTRIFIERS GO HOME on the sidewalk. Could a dog be a gentrifier? Not this one, she was perfect. She made me feel like I could be a mother. In the community bookstore I even felt well enough to buy my first ever copy of *Ariel*. Its cover was an unsettling color directly between red and orange that you couldn't identify as belonging to either. It felt like the kind of book someone serious would buy in a bookstore where everything was annoyingly expensive. *Ariel* was cheap. Sometimes you don't have a choice; you have to identify with a white woman.

Back in the dogsitting apartment, I read, "In these poems, written in the last months of her life, Sylvia Plath becomes herself—" That felt rude to say, that someone became themselves right as they decided they had had enough. I shut the book and held it away from me, disgusted by the past, like I always was. I missed my boyfriend but still I was in too good of a mood. I loved my dogsitting dog. I knew, as an absolute truth of the universe, that if I stole her and brought her home with me, my life would be perfect.

All week, she kept my cup three-quarters full. I didn't understand as a child, shirking chores, but: walking a dog can bring you to new places. Chicago, it was cool. I saw three cars with cartoon flames. The church towers wore scaffolding like a suburban woman in a spa, microneedles stuck into her face. They would emerge in the spring refreshed, pampered. But you could still see that the building was a church. It would always be a church, no matter what state of disrepair it was in.

No matter how much the church told itself one day it would be converted into an Urban Outfitters, the teens inside it would never be able to fully enjoy their flirting, their stealing, their vaping in the dressing room, they would always have the feeling that they were in God's presence—the dog pulled me away from the church, not comprehending metaphor, or not giving a shit. She pulled me away, out of the poem, toward whatever was out of her reach; everything that makes up the world has its own distinct smell, she was saying.

JOHNNY TEACHES ME HOW TO USE
A POWER DRILL IN REVERSE

to drive the screws out of his work desk, so we can fit it
down his basement staircase. Then he teaches me how
to drill the screws in again and we put it back together
together. In the basement he teaches me how to hold a drumstick.
He holds my hand and starts up a rhythm for me, my arms
slack but on beat—a metaphor so clear it's sickening—
on my back porch he teaches me how to put air in my bike tires,
and later I let him show me how to cut the seeds out of a jalapeno,
stubborn and glad when he stops me from touching my own eye
just as I was about to touch it. Sometimes in bed he puts the palm of his
hand on my chest and says something like, what if we let your feelings
in, instead, and I say, let them into *where*? When he spins me
around in his living room sometimes I spin the wrong way—
Apparently I was supposed to know what it meant
when he left his toothbrush at my apartment.
I am supposed to stay still and let him pick the crust
from my eyes in the morning. At night I let him see me
with my hair tied up. I lie in bed next to him and read,
just read. It's not that bad, I guess, letting my feelings in.
Today he's teaching me how to paddle a canoe.
You don't have anything to worry about, he says.
I feel the boat rocking beneath me
but I keep my elbow straight like his.
We're sweethearts, he says, against the sunset—
and I become the me in the middle of this lake—

ELECTION DAY,

thinking about how I missed the bus to Philadelphia for the sixth-grade trip. It was supposed to be a four days' long. We were going to learn about America. I had an upset stomach because I was scared. I couldn't get on the bus—something bad might happen. On it, in front of everyone. In retrospect my nerves were part of a pattern. I would be avoiding groups of people in enclosed spaces for years to come. I hadn't yet learned to deal with the shame of being different. Sometimes things that were easy for what-felt-like everyone were difficult for me. My peers could all easily get on a bus to Philadelphia, for example. Humiliating, still, sometimes. I was crying—for drama's sake, probably, in the top bunk of my bunk beds. My cries must have floated mom-ward in an especially pathetic way because she summoned up enough sympathy to drive me there herself. It was only an hour and forty-five minutes away, but I couldn't believe my mother had that level of love in her. I took it as if it might become her norm. I hadn't learned that lesson yet either. The entire drive to Philadelphia, I read Al Franken's *Rush Limbaugh Is a Big Fat Idiot and Other Observations*. The entire Philadelphia trip, I read Al Franken. I read Al Franken at the firehouse-themed restaurant. My chicken sandwich was dry. I was thirteen and this was the third Al Franken book I'd read. I feel on Election Day these facts become obvious about me: I can't help but care. I well up in the voting booth. How many times had I seen the black candidate hug his close friend, a cop? He never once said defund the police, he swore, in 30-second spots. I remember seeing the Liberty Bell and feeling disappointed.

ELEGY

After my students leave the classroom, I barely talk to anyone
for the rest of the week; six days only saying *thank you*
to the woman at the deli for slicing half a pound of roasted turkey,
double-checking the math on my tip with the girl working takeout
at the Indian restaurant, giving the finger to the driver who doesn't stop
to let me cross the street. Politely asking the ticket attendant
to print my movie ticket, so I can add it to my collection, smiling
at the man on the train who mouths *cool tattoos*. Exchanging
a nod with the black woman at the Jimmy Carter Presidential Library
holding the door as I enter the museum. The black woman
nodding *Hello, Sister*, as I head in to see the First Lady's body.
The silence I exchange with the soldier standing over her.
The fake monarchs flying through the flowers on her casket—
It almost made me cry. The way I thought to myself, *that's my friend!*
as her hearse's motorcade passed me on the street today, waving.

TO NYC SASHA:

Don't freak out
but you're fat again.
It's okay; I found us
jeans that fit. I visited
the Carter Center.
It was the first time
we didn't hate the president more
after the museum. Don't worry,

he's going to die
soon. I'll wait in line
to see the body for us.
The body is temporary.
We're lucky,
believe me?

IT'S SO IDYLLIC HERE

until you realize no one else cares about the new *Mission Impossible* movie. It's safe to walk alone at night. Past the park where the Boston Symphony Orchestra plays, via livestream, to a crowd of picnic blankets, to the ice-cream stand, and back.

The best week of my life was the week I discovered Talking Heads *and* weed. And the documentary about the grown-up boy-evangelist, preaching for money. And now I'm bored.

Annoying: the car that pulls up next to me in traffic playing, at full volume, seagull noises. I flip the sign in front of the free fruit tray that says TAKE SOME! And write:

THIS IS A RECIPE FOR BUGS. Tonight's the opposite of a full moon: an empty moon.

People are bad. Except the one girl I saw pause to throw the tennis ball back over the fence.

The fruit tray's gone the next day. Then there's a bird's nest in the O of the Taco Bell sign. I wait, listening for baby birds.

I can hear the employees arguing about colorism. It makes me think, maybe the seagull sounds were just the sea. Does that make sense? That's how bad of a mood I've been in.

If you forced me, I would say thank you to the Neanderthals, but only for inventing kissing.

Doesn't *pith* sound like a poem word? I peeled pith from my orange in the dark theater.

I'M STARTING TO LIKE THIS VERSION OF MYSELF, ACTUALLY,

so I'm not going to apologize for driving poorly
in the Target parking lot at 2 p.m. on a Monday.
Now that I don't live in New York City anymore
I don't think I should have to run into anyone
on a sidewalk or in a parking lot—
though a girl I knew there keeps posting online
about how she only eats raw meat now, and how she didn't vote.
"Breast cancer is God's way of showing the female body
how much it can do," she chatters into her front-facing camera
—I can't unfollow her,

I like things that are bad for me too much.
I got my first fake tan last week. For a second
I forgot to put the sunglasses in my eyes and looked
directly into the wall of UV lights. Today it's overcast.
I am a bad driver. I had a teacher in high school
who was always tripping over her brown maxi dress
and getting into minor car crashes while writing poems.
"Another little fender bender!" she sang to our restless class.
If I ever thought I would never be like that I was wrong.
Now all I want is when I make a mistake
for everyone to say, "Oh, Sasha! Her mistakes
are so spectacular we can't seem to look away!"
Like how I'm trying to learn how to be assertive,
but I keep coming off as aggressive instead. Like
I screamed, "Who are you calling girl?" at a man
in a bar. "Do you see any girls here?" I said,
gesturing up and down my own body. "Do you?"

The storm kept holding off, so I decided
to get ice cream. The door was steamed up
and the line was out the door. The girl in front of me didn't tip
then turned around and said, "I love your tattoos!"

I didn't want her compliments because I don't like people
who don't tip, and I actually said that to her, I didn't hold it in,
I didn't walk home licking my waffle cone in shame.

NO FAP FOUND POEM
from *reddit.com/r/nofap*

This is how my upward spiral starts:
another day one in the books.
I place a dollar in a jar every morning.
I am paying myself not to _____.
Porn is for losers. I used to be a loser.
I water my pot of wheatgrass.
I check on our growth together.
I ask myself, *what could you send out
into this world other than semen?*

The urges are strong but so am I. Instead of
_____, I went for a walk by the river. Instead of
_____, I auditioned for the local community theater
production of *Seussical*. I landed the role of Horton,
the elephant. I spent the day in the mountains.
I reclaimed my manhood. I let myself think about porn
in the forest. I imagined sex as nonlinear, and it scared me.
Don't question the science behind a COLD SHOWER,
just take one. You want science? After seven days without
_____, the testosterone levels leap. After a month,
I grew my first beard. At two months, I properly administered CPR
and saved my mother's life. At ninety days, I was like a leopard
escaped from the zoo, roaming the city with a limb in my mouth,
her fingernails painted gold. Instead of _____, I am learning German.
I deleted Snapchat. I had the energy to make lasagna. I built a robot.
Instead of _____, a photo of the sunrise, instead of _____,
a photo from the nosebleeds, instead of _____, a self portrait,
an elaborate Lego structure. A jog through Manhattan.
I was thinking I might buy recording equipment and write a song, instead.

I would like to stop resetting. Rome burned in a day,
I could think of myself as Rome. I could think
of myself as someone who touches someone else.

In the break room, I got so turned on watching her dip
her tea bag into a mug. Cranberry tea.
The water kept turning pinker and pinker
but instead of _____, I went back to my desk
and sketched this astronaut.

GRUDGE PERSON

We always say we're whatever people, like we're Bob Seger people because we listened to "Night Moves" four times in a row then twice in the morning, or we're e-bike people after that weekend with the e-bikes, Billy Joel people, cleaver people, mini golf people, but when he said we're co-op people! I said, no, don't even joke about that, and then I told him about back when I worked there, and how one time when, after catching a white shoplifter, my supervisor came running up to my lane, leaned his lanyard over my belt, and said, *See? we don't only get black people for shoplifting here.*

My boyfriend's eyes lifted up in a way that made me think the story was worse than I thought, like maybe we should put down our ginger shots and get out of there. But it's almost ten years later now, so I shop at the co-op again. I refuse to smile back when that supervisor smiles at me, still full-time, welcoming me to the store, shifting his hips back and forth in the rollie chair behind the customer service desk. It's fine, not forgiving. You don't have to forgive anybody for anything. So much racist stuff has happened to me here, the town I choose to live in. The street I choose to work on. The café where I pick up shifts. Last shift alone a man asked me if he could take a photo of me to show to his granddaughter. She looked like me; he wanted her to see. See what?

And then the tall guy who owned the vintage shop across the street came into the café with his mother. He introduced me to her as someone who is obsessed with the presidents, which I am. Her name was Val, so I picked her out the Scrabble mug with a V on it for her coffee. When I went back to the kitchen to tell the cook the story of the last time I talked to the vintage shop owner, the cook told me Val was in town because their mutual friend had died. That's the kind of town this is: everyone knows why you're in town. Everyone knows the truth about what kind of person you are.

They let it slide because they love the things you sell. About
six years ago, outside a cocktail bar, the vintage shop owner and
I were flirting. He asked me what was up. I said, nothing really,
just I think we have fleas in my apartment, and he said, well I
hope you don't have any fleas in here, then raised both his hands
and stuck them into my hair. He held my head, shaking imaginary
fleas out of my afro. I know your eyebrows are raised right now.
You wouldn't blame me if I couldn't forgive him.

But if you were one of my female friends back then, you
probably would have said, well I would still fuck him. Or if you
lived in town in 2016, and I was sitting on the floor of your living

room, each of us smoking our own joint, sending a walking wind-
up toy shaped like a human ear back and forth to each other across
your low coffee table—if I said where did you get this walking
ear, and you said, at the vintage shop owner's shop, I would have
told you the flea story, but it would only ruin the walking ear for
you very temporarily. It would regain its cuteness and its kitsch
shortly after I left your apartment. But like I said, no one here
knows how to hold a grudge—

Maybe you do. It's a shame about the flea conversation,
especially because the week before, I was actually considering
fucking the vintage shop owner—he had found me at a different
bar to give me a gift. He lit my cigarette and handed me a plastic
bag. Inside were four soft doll heads and a headless doll. The
doll was dressed like a boxer, in wristbands and American flag
shorts, abs printed across its hairy chest. Each head belonged to
a different candidate from the 1992 presidential election. Ross
Perot's little glasses were so cute. Clinton's face was off-center.

The doll's neck was Velcroed so you could rip off and reattach
different heads, depending on who you wished would win.

He had stopped me, outside the cocktail bar that night, before putting his hands in my hair, to tell me he found a missing piece of the doll.

He tipped a hundred and twenty percent on his breakfast today. I said have a great day the same way I would have to anyone, without meaning it. He walked his mom to her car; I watched him kiss her hand, her forehead. She drove off and he went into his shop. The front window of the shop was set with an arrangement of unique lamps; my favorite had bulbs shaped like seashells. I had never been inside. The cook called order up, and I went back to serving. The bell rang on the door. The vintage shop owner had come back: with the doll's missing Velcro heart.

He said, *I've been keeping the president's heart for you, in a bag, in a drawer, since the last time I saw you.* He didn't say anything like forgive me? before he handed it over, but I heard how the heart sang with it.

I THOUGHT MY LIFE WAS OVER

I thought my life was over but it was only a pandemic.
I fled the city, I couldn't even sleep there one more night.
It was March 13th. I fell asleep in my suburb,
Breonna Taylor fell asleep in her city. Now
that she's dead, I know these details about her life.
She was going to turn 26 on June 5th, I was going to turn 30.
I didn't want to. I wasn't eating, but I had to shop.
I only went downstairs to wipe off my packages.
I overheard my father on a phone call with his doctor
who was saying, "Yes, for now, you're still prediabetic." For now.
For a week I thought about his belly crushing his lungs.
Somehow, his sixty-eighth birthday passed. I didn't kill him,
but we didn't hug. I kept preparing myself to lose.
I prepared myself to see so many dead black people.
Historically, I had to be prepared. I collected unemployment
while I complained. I was practically chanting it.
My life is over. Hers was. All those years
we celebrated together and didn't know it.
In my dreams, I wished for a birthday party.
I was wearing a pink feathered robe, I was the center of attention,
I was the piece of shit—why did I get to live?
I thought my life was over but it kept going.

JOY IS MY MIDDLE NAME

"Each moment and whatever happens thrills me with joy,
I cannot tell how my ankles bend, nor whence the cause
of my faintest wish"
—Walt Whitman, *Leaves of Grass*

I hold my fingers to my neck like a pair of lips. Joy is my middle name!
Joy is my middle name,

can it please feel like that for once! I don't want to check my pulse this
much! I want a life full of ice-fishing holes!

Joy the first time I stepped inside a frat house, a real frat house, and
it was so like a movie I thought maybe the whole world wasn't a lie.
There was even a red Solo cup frozen into the snow!

I looked at the clock and it was 12:46. I ran through the whole party to
find Ian, shook him: "It's 12:46 and we're at twelve forty-six College
Street!!" That was real joy. 10:10. 11:11. Little joyful

coincidences. You don't know me if you've never heard me squeal. At
ice-fishing holes! In extended child's pose! Three yellow shovels! I
want joy, but like my horoscope always says:

You will struggle with addiction. But I'm not drinking right now! The
virtual log rolling event went on as planned! I fold tiny paper airplanes
out of scrap paper I was wired exactly right!

Joy is my mother

fucking middle name! It was another normal day until Pete texted,
"Wanna smoke?" at 7 a.m. and the squeal I let out!

I brought down a raspberry seltzer for him and he brought me
a shot of espresso. It wasn't normal, it was the first day over 30 degrees
all month—!

I spent ten years cultivating an extensive array of weed tricks. Sure, I
was depressed, but I never Had Depression. I watched my childhood
dog die! I heard him yelp

and still my middle name was Joy.

If you think you want to experience excess like this, you can start by
noticing when your oatmeal water and your coffee water come to boil
together.

Don't just stand there!
Run for your notebook! Stir weave stretch breathe a brighter and
clearer joy! Smile O voluptuous cool-breath'd joy!

Joy of the slumbering and liquid trees! Joy of departed sunset—smile,
for your joy comes!

The forklift driver I dated worked fourteen-hour shifts! He said he
thought about my body the whole time. The thought of him stretching
the thought of my body to last fourteen hours, starting

with my pinky toenail (!) and working his way up from there, Oh My
God, he was 6 foot 5! We broke a Motel 6 bed! Tangerine is finally in!
Joy is in! Let it in! Stop telling me you know how I feel when you don't!

POEM AFTER MOVING AWAY

I just got carded at the movies. Tonight
I'll stand over my tiny shower
and detangle my tangled hair. My students
are mostly writing about gun violence
and girlhood. My steering wheel
keeps shaking when I brake. I'm wearing
my middle school softball sweatshirt a lot.
I received an email inviting me to a BIPOC
affinity group for adults. I headed off campus
for ice cream. The cows grazed as I licked
my chocolate cone. I keep one sunscreen
in my hallway and one sunscreen in my car.
I eat falafel at the food carts. Cross
the street to get closer to the water. I miss
the lake behind my apartment. Far, far
away. Now a new girl lives there,
only 22, a year younger than me
when I moved to Madison:
I got my first real job, biked two blocks,
skidded to an awkward stop and skinned
my knee on Willy Street. Sometimes
I biked to the bakery for a fresh filled roll,
but only one oozing chorizo. I biked
behind my first real drug dealer, his tires
lit and spinning pink in my first real Midwestern
summer storm. I was barely 23.
My arms filled up with tattoos. The bars filled
up around me. The bartender spilled my shot
and bought me a new one. In my old
apartment, where we kissed for the first time,
the girl who lives there is definitely
doing her dishes before bed. She's opening
the door to the back deck and listening
to the lake. The lake's alive and slivering

up the rock. The rocks are probably something like twenty trillion years old.

POEM FOR THE RACIST TOUR GUIDE
AT THE FRANKLIN PIERCE MANSE

I dragged my poor little exhausted plaque-slut heart
across much of New Hampshire yesterday,
even stopping off at PRESIDENT PIERCE HIGHWAY
for a TWIN SET OF HAND-CRAFTED STONE BRIDGES,
SUSTAINED SOLELY BY EXPERT SHAPING
OF ARCHSTONES, TYPICAL
OF THE FIRST HALF OF THE 19th CENTURY.
"Is it pronounced ARCH or ARCH? You know,
I simply *adore* the first half of the nineteenth century,"
I said to the plaque. I was flirting.
It was a beautiful plaque.
It took me about one hour and forty-five minutes
to drive from my hotel to Pierce's birthplace,
Pierce's home, Pierce's grave,
barely paying attention to the road—
embarrassing for him, for whom his
life seemed so difficult.
Hillsborough is spelled sometimes
ending with a *gh* and sometimes
ending with an *o*, like *Hillsboro!*
maybe to lighten the mood of the place.
WELCOME TO HILLSBORO,
BIRTHPLACE OF OUR 14th PRESIDENT
FRANKLIN PIERCE.
OUR, says the sign.
A series of delicate white arrows
pointed me to his grave:
NATIVE SON OF NEW HAMPSHIRE,
COURAGEOUS ADVOCATE OF STATE'S RIGHTS,
LIES BURIED IN A NEARBY ENCLOSURE.
None of the signs said BLEEDING KANSAS,
none said FUGITIVE SLAVE ACT,
I just knew. *Shame!* they screamed in Boston,

as police dragged FUGITIVE SLAVES to jail.
Someone wrote "Spring Eternal!"
on the bottom of a rock painted with birds
and left it there. I tucked the rock
between my pinky and ring finger.
Hunched over my trunk, I wrapped it in a dirty sock.
I pulled up to the FRANKLIN PIERCE statue hoping
it would have been pulled down, considering
everything he'd done,
but instead the sun was setting, setting
a sort of glow across the statue's face
making him look, honestly, handsome.
I wrote *shame* in my little black notebook.
The cover of the notebook said
FRANKLIN PIERCE, JULY 2020.
I had written it in gold Sharpie,
which was already smudging.
50,000 people screaming *Shame!*
while police loaded FUGITIVE SLAVES
on to the southern-bound ships,
and all I do is study the nineteenth century.
I think dumb little thoughts
about the black people buried
in the cemetery with Pierce.
Not particularly helpful thoughts, either,
thoughts like, what if
we moved his body somewhere
it can't hurt anyone?
I pulled over at FRANKLIN PIERCE LAKE
but I didn't think it was worth
getting out of the car to touch the water.
I had to pee, and I thought touching water
would make me need to pee more.
Instead I held my pee for good,
downtown again, waiting for my to-go order;
enough chicken wings to eat some cold for breakfast.

I ate the fries on the drive back to the hotel.
I used my greasy hand to write down all the signs I saw:
GROOVED SHOULDERS! MOOSE CROSSING!
RUMBLE STRIPS! WET LINES! MOOSE! again.
BE ALERT! BE PREPARED TO TOP!
Someone had scratched out the S.
BIKE-FRIENDLY COMMUNITY
said the blue sign at the edge of Concord,
with its painted red heart.
Its dead president. I could never stop
thinking but I really couldn't stop thinking
that Franklin Pierce statue
was awfully close to the street.
It pleased me to imagine a car exactly like mine
driving into it. I thought it would be funny
if they buried it with its head down.
And more than that? I wanted a plaque.
One that told the truth. Maybe two plaques.
Or four, to really surround it. It would be easy.
Cheap. I wanted a world where you could really look
at yourself, and I wanted the statue's handsome evil
racist little mouth, full of dirt.

WHEN I MET SHARON OLDS SHE TOLD ME TO WRITE A POEM ABOUT LBJ'S PENIS

Everyone in my family knew
how horny I was long before I did.
At my grandmother's funeral
I remembered fondly the time
she caught me looking at porn
over her dial-up. I humped
her basement floor watching *BET Uncut*.
Music videos had the most sex. Women
bent over and covered in cash,
conquered. At home my mother slept
on the couch, I sat upstairs
on the corner of her bed, flipping
through channels, looking for sex.
I was desperate to see a penis.
I didn't want to write the poem.
What's so poetic
about a sad man pulling proof
out of his pants, windmilling
his dick backward into his own grave?
What color could you even
compare him to? I remember
my elementary school gym teacher
laughing at his own punchline,
some joke about touching yourself.
I knew the joke was about sex
so I kept my questions to myself.
Wouldn't it be impossible to not
touch yourself? I think I might be
touching myself right now?
I assumed everyone knew
that whenever LBJ felt stupid
or upstaged or small, he took
his penis out. He slammed it

on the table. My life changed
when I found out what I could do
with my mouth. I licked
it all up, thirsty as any lifelong learner,
any other lover of the last drop,
swallowing everything but
what I had to say. I bragged
with the bombs I was given.
I dropped them exactly when
I wanted. Rules were only odes to order,
suggestions with a playful grip on the throat.
Every time a couple fights
about me, I get tighter.
My pussy ruined a marriage,
led them back to each other
and blessed them with a son.
My body count is growing. Gather
the video girls. Tell them to twerk to this:
LBJ is in hell with all the other presidents!
On a burning hilltop, in a graveyard
full of flaccid legacies, they wave
their penises like white flags.

I WENT OUT TO SEE ALL THE DOWNED TREES

Nothing was where it was supposed to be
or even where it was twenty minutes ago,
one of the only times I've understood
what nature was trying to say
to me. But the people I always see
at the farmers' market being very specific
about their mushroom selection weren't
listening, already dragging branches
onto the curb, fixing their lawns,
resetting their Black Lives Matter signs
these were the people blasting
"Celebrate good times, come on!"
from their front porch windows
on the day Joe Biden was elected.
One of them was high-fiving
a police officer. The branches were still green,
on the ground. The sun hadn't browned
the dead leaves yet. There was part
of me that trusted them, my neighbors.
I hadn't locked my door when I left.
One neighbor said, I hired an arborist
just a few weeks ago, and he said
this tree was fine. The neighbor
motioned toward a tree currently
pulling back power lines down
on top of their red Subaru.
I took a picture of the crushed car,
didn't hide my snicker. Who
could afford an arborist?
I would never own a house,
or a tree, or my own car.
But these were neighbors, and we
had to clean this up together.

IF YOU WANNA JUST SAY FUCK IT

and get me pregnant, then fuck it,
I'll take out my IUD right here and do it,
give my hormones what they want—

small house, walkable city,
permanent end to my uselessness—
Fuck it, take me. Imagine: I'm pregnant,

everyone worshipping me,
leaving ripe peaches at my feet.
Honey on the doorstep. Round, halo

tummy, long flowing dresses, exhaustive
lists of riotous demands, absolutely
brimming with boundless entitlement.
Being pregnant is the only thing
that will stop me from thinking

about being pregnant. I'll drink
non-alcoholic beer for free all summer
while wearing an absurdly large-brimmed

hat. I'll have three large-brimmed hats.
I'll seem to grow an inch taller. At sunset,
we'll foam roll in silence together. You'll put

your hand on my growing stomach
and we'll inhale and exhale in unison.
I wanna be pregnant so bad

it almost makes me forget
how bad of a mother I'll probably be.
Whatever, bend me over. Fuck

me. I've got a boyfriend but
he doesn't take me seriously.
I'd be perfect as a pregnant woman,

finally taking up the space
I've always been meant to.
You'll kiss my forehead

at the farmers' market. At the co-op
we'll be nice to the cashiers.
We'll over-tip. I'll wear overalls.

Labor will be painless. You'll tell me
how beautiful I am all the time,
looking up from the garden

where you're kneeling
in the dirt, planting carrots
and squash and kale

and other things I'll blend
into baby food (The baby.
Her little curls. I see it.)

and spoon into individual
plastic containers. As a family
we'll throw away approximately

400 pounds of plastic per year.
We'll learn to ski. She'll love
the library. She'll be tall enough

to play basketball but we won't
pressure her. We'll go through
the car wash together and sing

our car wash song, *sh-sh-sh*-ing in time
with the fabric on the windshield.
She'll be 45 percent you, 45 percent me,

10 percent microplastics, but
we'll love her as if she were
100 percent human,

just like our parents tried to. I can't wait
to love her. On walks, I go blocks
picturing her forehead. Last week

on an especially long one down
University Avenue, I saw an excavator
tearing down an old campus building.

The closer I got to the building,
the more it became obvious the claw was
only nipping at its innards, taking

away what it could hold in its messy,
puppeted mouth. It wasn't violent at all.
I watched it, pulling, slowly dismantling

the fourth, fifth, sixth floor, readying it
all to be rebuilt, I thought, I could be
pregnant, it can't be that bad. Fuck it.

DEBTS, SOURCES, NOTES
after Robert Caro

The "CENTO FOR THE NIGHT I TRIED STAND-UP" (inspired by Nicole Sealey's "Cento for the Night I Said, 'I Love You'") features lines from (kind of in order of appearance—I did my best): Stewart Lee, Mike Birbiglia, Demetri Martin, Jerrod Carmichael, Romesh Ranganathan, Ed Gamble, Bill Hicks, Daniel Tosh, Richard Pryor, John Mulaney, Bernie Mac, Katt Williams, Neal Brennan, James Acaster, Nate Bargatze, Sean Lock, Andy Zaltzman, Richard Herring, Maria Bamford, Rory Scovel, Frankie Boyle, Nish Kumar, Dave Attell, Nicole Byer, Mitch Hedberg, Jim Gaffigan, Simon Munnery, Chris Rock, David O'Doherty, John Oliver, Tig Notaro, Todd Barry, Kyle Kinane, Tim Heidecker, Roy Wood, Jr., Joe Mande, Dulcé Sloan, Paul F. Tompkins, Brody Stevens, Moms Mabley, Kumail Nanjiani, , Joe Lycett, Reggie Watts, Amy Schumer, Louie Anderson, Patton Oswalt, Elizabeth Aziz. I consider many of these people to have had a significant impact on my voice and on my poetry, especially Stewart Lee. I lay in my bed as a teenager and listened to my Dane Cook and Daniel Tosh CDs over and over; using them in this poem is my admitting to that. My influences are not always pure. One day I will deliver a thoughtful lecture on this topic (no I won't), but to put it simply: I believe poetry and stand-up are the same, except stand-up routines take the audience's enjoyment into consideration. Also, stand-ups don't try and hide the fact that, at their core, they only want to be liked.

Wanda Coleman wrote "my metaphor my life" in her poem, "Ms. Pac Man." The poem begins: "video fever comes late. i am found."

Lyndon Johnson clarified that the "yelp is not a sound of pain" on May 2, 1964, after animal rights activists were upset that he lifted his beagle up by its ears and said he liked to "hear [dogs] yelp." I found this in "Quotations from Chairman LBJ," which I bought on a 2007 trip to New York City.

I filmed myself having a crying breakdown while trying to French braid my own hair in March 2020, at the beginning of the Covid-19 pandemic. In "YOUR BRAIN IS NOT A PRISON!" I can French braid my hair. If you can't do something you can write yourself doing it and that counts too.

The "overheard" epigraph from "SAMPLE OF MYSELF" is something my most beloved reader and best friend Peach told me Anne Carson said, but it seemed inappropriate to quote Anne Carson here, because I do not even know who Sappho is and at this point I'm too scared to ask. One Saturday in February 2020, a woman sampled out vegan Bloody Mary mix in the upscale butcher shop in Williamsburg in Brooklyn where I worked the register. (My second upscale butcher shop job.) She was standing five feet away from me and described the mix as "artisanal, organic, award-winning, vegan, gluten-free" with the same exact intonation, to every single person who sampled the Bloody Mary mix, for about four hours. She told them to "roll it around [their] mouth and make sure it hits every point of the palate."

I have a tattoo on my left forearm that says "2 Furious." My friend Claire (@snaggletoothtattoo on Instagram) did it, after tattooing "2 Fast" on someone I don't know. It was the last tattoo I got in Wisconsin before I moved home in 2017 and weaned myself off antidepressants. While withdrawing from sertraline, I had to drive to work (at a shitty Italian restaurant in West Hartford, Connecticut) at sunset and the windshield glare plus light and shadows through the leaves plus the fact I couldn't turn my head left or right without experiencing brain zaps made the drive almost impossible. Plus, I was probably stoned and crying over one of the love songs on the Garth Brooks tape that played constantly in my 1997 teal Chevy Lumina. I worked at that restaurant for six months, and at month five my co-worker told me that he used to breed rabbits as a teenager. I love learning stuff like that about people; once I worked with a line cook who was an extreme couponer. I quit the Italian place because I overheard one bartender say to another, "Dude there's a lesbian couple at the bar tonight and they're actually hot for once." ("'FAST & FURIOUS' Stars' Complicated Demand—I Never Want to Lose a Fight," Erich Schwartzel, *The Wall Street Journal*, 2019). This poem originally appeared in *Granta*.

The doctor from "WHAT AM I AFRAID OF?" really did say this stuff. And so did the woman, about the kale, and the man outside the butcher shop (my first upscale butcher shop job). But a lot of the things I say people said in this book they didn't really say. This poem was written after my friend died, the poet April Freely. Hi, April.

White people like the "SESTINA" so much more than I do. I don't think it's mean enough to LBJ. It was published in *The Yale Review*, January 2020, my first big publication. The morning the issue came out I had so much excitement in my body that I walked from 94th on the Upper East Side all the way down to the West Village. In my mind, the "SESTINA" and "JORDAN" are both basically "after" "MATT" by Morgan Parker. Thank you Morgan Parker.

It felt like my friend imogen was in the room with me when I wrote "RACIST BONE." That's why I let myself write like that. "I jump at the sight of my shadow every single day" is not an exaggeration. Well, not the biggest exaggeration I've ever made. A Black Manhattan replaces the sweet vermouth with Averna. My sobriety is all over the place in this book, but I had a beautiful Granny Manhattan phase in 2016. Granny Manhattans are two parts sweet vermouth, one part rye. The relevant facts are sourced from the National Museum of Civil War Medicine's website. Frog Hollow is a neighborhood near the South End of Hartford. Stonewall Jackson's arm is buried in Locust Grove, Virginia. I sprinkle salt on all my ice cream before I eat it.

I do not believe in the "DEATH PENALTY." When I refer to

"Birmingham," I'm referring to the 1963 Baptist Street Church bombing that killed Addie Mae Collins (14), Cynthia Dionne Wesley (14), Carole Rosamond Robertson (14), and Carol Denise McNair (11). From 2011–2022 I had no boyfriend. "In 1936, the [Federal Writers' Project] began collecting interviews with former slaves, amassing thousands of pages of oral histories which, though often filtered through the racism of white interviewers and their supervisors, provide an invaluable snapshot of how more than 2,000 survivors of slavery lived and thought. Nearly 40 of those interviewed claimed Abraham Lincoln visited their plantation shortly before or during the Civil War. They said he came in disguise as a beggar or a peddler, bummed free meals off his unsuspecting white hosts, snooped around to find out what slavery was like, and told the slaves they would soon be free." ("Abraham Lincoln's Secret Visits to Slaves," William R. Black, *The Atlantic*, 2018.) Robert Kennedy said, "For those of you who are black and are tempted to be filled with hatred and distrust at the injustice of such an act, against all white people, I can only say that I feel in my own heart the same kind of feeling. I had a member of my family killed, but he was killed by a white man," on April 4, 1968, in Indianapolis. He was announcing the death of Martin Luther King, Jr., to the crowd. These poems originally appeared in *TriQuarterly*.

I feel kind of bad about the things I say about my mom in "KAEPERNICK," but I also think this poem is good. I love you, Mom, I'm sorry. There is only one thing I would never write about, and you'll never know what it is. After a full year of limbo, this poem was picked out of the slush pile and published in *The* actual *New Yorker*.

The first time I read "BIOPIC" out loud I thought the audience would think it was hilarious, but I could tell, about halfway through, they thought it was sad whoops. I think of it as part of a pair with "STAND-UP ROUTINE." The biopic in my mind was Baz Luhrmann's *Elvis*.

Do you guys kinda feel like I ripped off the last line of "GAIN

WEIGHT" from "Our Song" by Taylor Swift? I'd be okay with it if you did. Actually, Taylor, if you're reading this, can I say thank you for helping me value sentimentality in my own work? I love you. Do you want to write a song together? Or a poem? I'm imagining it would like how Miller Williams gave Jimmy Carter poetry lessons. This poem originally appeared in *bath magg*.

The Packer game I "PRAY"ed over was the 2022 NFC Divisional Playoff. The San Francisco 49ers won 13–10. The beer was a Hinterland Packerland Pilsner. The man was Johnny, who has the same birthday as Abraham Lincoln. My favorite baseball player was Torii Hunter. I saw him steal a home run away from Barry Bonds in the 2002 All-Star Game and fell in love. I wrote his initials all over my mother's house in black Sharpie: TKH, TKH, TKH. I don't pray to God, I ask my angels for favors. This poem originally appeared in *The New York Review of Books*.

I love working in restaurants. Working a busy shift at a restaurant is like wringing your brain out like a towel. You get good stories. And bad stories, like "LIKE." I do not "get" Wes Anderson movies, but he was the funniest possible director I could have named. Sometimes you have to make compromises. This poem originally appeared in *The Yale Review*.

My one real piece of advice for young writers is do not go directly to graduate school after college. Instead, you need to have experiences like the ones I'm talking about in "LOOKING BACK." This poem is for everyone I drank with on Willy Street, but especially Anna Sisson, my best friend, our one brain. She'd agree: I could have swapped out "Torn" for "Linger" or "Crash Into Me," but those didn't add any consonance to the poem.

I got the "fear itself" tattoo in "WART" in downtown Beloit, Wisconsin, where I attended college from January 2009 through May 2013. I was a Creative Writing major and an

American Studies minor. I think I was one of the last two American Studies minors. Emily (who I did karaoke with in Joshua Tree) and Megan (inventor of the infamous Megantini: vodka, Red Bull, Emergen-C) were there when I got the tattoo, but I can't remember which one held my hand. I used the presidents placemat image and the FDR museum memory in countless poems I wrote in high school and at Beloit, but now this is published in *Nashville Review* and in this book so I can't use them anymore. I thank them for their service. Terrance Hayes was like, "What if this poem was one sentence?" My wart did eventually go away. My patriotism is complicated. Mostly ironic. But I do feel it sometimes, quickly, like twisting the top off a High Life bottle. Like scooping up a toad. Like an otter popping its head out of the lily pads. My patriotism is like: my high school locker, a porta-potty with the word AMERICANS in red, white, and blue across it, and all the drugs I've ever stolen from white men, piled up in a vault for me to dive into. The New Britain parties where everyone sang "Happy Birthday" in Spanish, then a second time in Polish. Being part of a restaurant staff, drunk together in the back room of a karaoke bar. Irulan and Arissa smoking cigarettes in the lobby on *The Real World: Las Vegas.* Eleanor Roosevelt fingering her pistol's license, Derek Jeter diving into the stands at Yankee Stadium, A-Rod punched, on a loop. Two fat pugs curled up on a cheetah print couch. The Western Beef appearing in the distance. The road I ran down every morning named after the family that owned the last slave in Windsor. The summer at the diner I had all my regulars' breakfasts memorized. Over easy, bacon, rye toast. Teenagers cliff jumping at Indian Well Falls. Reading *Prozac Nation* at Mosquito Pond. The crane's perfect posture. The deserted car dealerships on Poquonuck. Christ Church Cathedral in Hartford, full for my grandmother's funeral.

The "CAT MARNELL" poem is the "NO FAP" poem, you know? One of my favorite genres of book is addiction memoir that doesn't end with the person getting their life together. That is the literary tradition I would like this book to be a part of.

The sister in "POLITICAL" "CONTAINER" is my sister Randa. My other sisters are DeeDee and Lynn. My brother's name is Evan, my father's name is Randy and my mother's name is Susan. Luke M. said he'd name a dog Mayonnaise during a date on season 6 of *Love Island*. This poem originally appeared in *TriQuarterly*.

I worked every "TUESDAY" with Blythe at Willalby's, a cash-only breakfast diner in Madison. My boss' name is Nate and we were both born on June 5th. I am a Gemini Sun, Scorpio Moon, and Scorpio Rising.

I stole *Real Housewives of New York City* "TAGLINES" from: Kelly, season 4; Ramona, season 5; Luann, season 1; Ramona, season 11; Bethenny, season 8; and Dorinda, season 10; but Carole is my favorite housewife, obviously.

I was in the "BERKSHIRES" because I was a resident at The Mastheads, a residency where I wrote in a studio at Herman Melville's Arrowhead. The five movies I saw there that summer were: *Top Gun Maverick* three times, *Elvis*, and *Nope*.

I wrote my "STAND-UP ROUTINE" during my deep obsession with Blank Check, a podcast about directors' filmographies. I didn't understand what directors did before I started listening to Blank Check. Now I know shit like, *Mission Impossible: Rogue Nation* was Christopher McQuarrie's first time directing a film in the series, and I can tell. I was watching a behind-the-scenes featurette from *Mission Impossible: Rogue Nation* about how Tom Cruise had to learn to hold his breath for six minutes to film the underwater scene, and when the man who taught him called it the "Breath Hold Special Operations Program," I paused the video and screamed and got up and walked a lap around my apartment because I was so excited about the prospect of using that in a poem one day. I never did so I'm talking about it here instead. This poem originally appeared in *Underblong*.

I finally don't have anything else to say about "JORDAN."

The Married Guy in "*NATIONAL TREASURE*" is from the couple I blessed with a baby in the "SHARON OLDS" poem, which means I blessed them with an ugly baby, so I don't know why I'm even bragging. MG lived at a pretty central intersection on a main street in Madison, Wisconsin, and I always made my friends drive down his street, so I could try to see him through his window, sitting at his desk. Once my friend Jodi gave me the brilliant advice to change his name in my phone to "Think About It." I've also used "Let It Go" and "DON'T TEXT." Beyonce's *Lemonade* came out while I was seeing MG so I didn't get to experience the album guilt-free and I will always hate him for taking that away from me. Is it really a first book if it doesn't have a sonnet in it? This poem originally appeared in *The Yale Review*.

The man in "*ALONE*DERLAND" is Tobias who "keeps a clog keychain on his keys that reminds him of French fries he ate in Amsterdam." I keep the pine cones from his parents' front yard on my living room table. I never made a bird friend. Season seven of *Alone* is the best season of television I have ever seen.

The bar in "CAT CALLED" is the Crown Inn in Crown Heights in Brooklyn, and nobody there saw the guy grab me. First he hit on me by saying, "I can tell you're a narcissist. I'm a narcissist too. That bond can be really strong." I was also getting harassed at work and was out at night drinking, trying to figure out if I could keep the job and deal with it. And then that guy grabbed my face. It was the first time a man had ever physically assaulted me and I quit my job the next week.

The poem that happened on "THE STREET IN WISCONSIN" didn't happen. I was sitting in BERG'N, the beer-hall-at-night-coffee-shop-during-the-day by my apartment in Brooklyn, trying to think of a simile for "ran through me like" and I looked up and saw the beer taps.

Ida McKenney was my grandmother. Her maiden name was Turner, and the Turners I came from come from Courtland, Virginia, which is where the Turners Nat Turner came from came from. Ida McKenney, June 16, 1936–May 21, 2018. According to her obituary she died at St Francis Hospital, I must have thought the two Hs sounded better. However: I was born at "HARTFORD HOSPITAL."

"JOHN BROWN" was born in Torrington, Connecticut. Frederick Douglass once said, "I could live for the slave, but [John Brown] could die for him . . . They could kill him but they could not answer him." There were multiple black men who lived in Windsor who fought in the US Colored Troops, and I never biked around looking in every cemetery, but the lady at the Windsor Historical Society did really say that the Civil War was too late in American history for them. Another thing that radicalized me was John M. McPherson's *The Negro's Civil War*, because it taught me the slaves freed themselves. People always talk about John Brown's rebellion like it's some complicated thing. It seems very simple to me. When I was watching Trump supporters storm the Capitol all I felt was jealously.

The song I sang at "KARAOKE" in Joshua Tree was "Trashy Women" by the band Confederate Railroad—which I heard for the first time on my supervisor's country music mix at Diner in Williamsburg in July 2018. It was my second ever time doing karaoke. The we in this poem is me and the Emily who was there when I got my "fear itself" tattoo. But the first time I sang karaoke was with a different Emily, in Madison, on New Year's Eve 2017. We sang "With Arms Wide Open" by Creed. I have had a major turnaround on karaoke and now I think it's cool and fun. My karaoke standards are "Friends in Low Places" by Garth Brooks and "I Love College" by Asher Roth. Both times I did "I Love College" at karaoke I got super laid (that's how I got the girl in AT 33,). When I think about how my life has changed because of the pandemic I think about how I once had sex in the bathroom at a karaoke bar. I put my bare ass on the sink.

Sometimes when I read my old tweets from when I drank a lot I think, oh, if I wasn't drinking so much that would have gone in a poem. So I started writing found poems using my old tweets. The letter referenced in "I am LITERALLY writing a letter I will never send to somebody who will never love me the way I want to be loved" could be about any of the approximately ten men referenced in this book, I have no idea. (It's definitely Jordan, but I said I wouldn't say more.) "Yoga to Calm Your Nerves" is a Yoga With Adriene YouTube video. Adriene is my mom. If she is your mom, too, we are related. The CD I broke was *Songs About Jane* by Maroon 5. I remember being so mad when the "Sunday Morning" video came out because I believed the music video would be me walking home from school. The black person I was crying about that day was Stuart Scott.

Pico, who I was "DOGSITTING" in Pilsen, belongs to my friends Bert and Mimi.

The lake "JOHNNY" and I were on is Lake Monona in Madison. The one behind my apartment. When I read this poem, I am there again. It was so weird, *Madison Magazine* reached out to ask if I had any love poems and I actually had one. My first love poem ever. Or, my first good one—I once wrote a love poem to my college boyfriend, comparing him to Ulysses S. Grant. The breakup poems about Johnny got cut out of the book so maybe in your mind we're still together, which is nice. I loved him so much I saw Phish five times with him. But we're not, so I'm sneaking one breakup poem back in:

I NEVER GOT TO SEE *DUNE 2* WITH JOHNNY

We'll never know how that story ends. Something always stopped us from foraging for morels. He never got to sauté them with butter for me. There was a woods by his parents' house we would have stalked together every spring, and after I'd've always needed him to tick check every inch of me. I never got to see his house painted mint green. Never got to watch the construction workers connect the house to the garage. Never did much more than water the raised beds once or twice, though I imagined myself planting something useful. Eventually would have learned the difference between a turkey vulture and a true hawk flying over us on the highway. Could have convinced him to try out for *Survivor*. I was going to remake the pumpkin bread pudding I brought to Thanksgiving last year, but better. Dessert was ruined when his parents' dog trotted in with a deer's bloody heart in her mouth. She placed the heart on the ground, so proud. And he got up and threw it out.

The black candidate in "ELECTION DAY" is Mandela Barnes. He lost. I took "mom-ward" from the poem "Language Lesson 1976" by Heather McHugh.

I'm scared to show any sympathy to any president, even to Jimmy Carter, the way I do in "TO NYC SASHA:" But the museums never work on me, I thought I was immune. AND YES, I wrote an "ELEGY" for Rosalynn Carter, and somehow it's the saddest poem I've ever written. They held her public funeral on Emory's campus in Atlanta, and Jimmy was in attendance.

The documentary about the "boy-evangelist" in "IT'S SO IDYLLIC" is *Marjoe* (like Mary and Joseph). Go watch it immediately, the book's basically over.

"ACTUALLY," I wrote this poem to show off to my former boss. I "ACTUALLY" slipped him my number but he never mentioned it and then I quit the restaurant like a month later because he sort of microaggressed me. It's shocking how many poems I write with the intention of showing them to a man, as if

my ability to write a poem will make them want to
sleep with me. (But would I keep doing it if it didn't
work?)

I found a lot of solace in the "NO FAP" subreddit the first
time I got sober. It's a deeply problematic forum whose
members truly believe you gain superpowers when you quit
masturbation. I kept thinking, like, shouldn't we all think we
develop superpowers when we overcome our addictions? My
current top five favorite subreddits are: r/bald, r/nattyorjuice,
r/icecream, r/shittyrestrictionfood and r/LoveIsland.

I feel like writing "GRUDGE PERSON" cured me of this
grudge. This was a failed prose poem I turned into "flash fiction"
(thank you to *The Greensboro Review*!) that I'm now trying to
pass off as a poem again. Willalby's is the diner, of course.

I did eventually have a huge 30th birthday party like the one I
wanted in "I THOUGHT MY LIFE WAS OVER" but I
had it on my 31st birthday. (Then, the day after my 31st birthday,
I had a 31st birthday party.) I wore pink (I did two outfit
changes) and I had donuts and ice-cream cake. My friend Emily
(a third Emily) and I spray painted a cornhole set hot pink. At
the end of the night, Johnny and I sat on the rocks by the lake
and poured an entire bottle of champagne out, into the lake, for
Breonna.

"JOY" is also my mother's middle name, but I was too scared
to bring that into the poem. My weed tricks are too sacred
to go into a poem, but I will say you should always layer the
kief in the middle of the bowl. I got to the point in Covid-19
lockdown where I made myself an intricate schedule and part
of that schedule was to read twenty minutes of *Leaves of Grass* at
4.20 p.m. every day. But then like I always do I tricked myself
into learning something. Bill Clinton gave *Leaves of Grass* to
every woman he ever "courted," including Hillary Clinton and
Monica Lewinsky. My mom gave a copy of Virginia Woolf's
A Room of One's Own to every guy she ever dated, including

my father. My copy of *Leaves of Grass* was a gift from Tobias'
parents. Some lines are stolen directly from Whitman. You can
tell which ones.

The bakery I "MOVED AWAY" from is Batch Bakehouse
in Madison. The filled roll there is the number-one hangover
cure in the world. The bartender I'm imagining is Ricky at the
Crystal Corner. He's the only bartender in the world as far as
I'm concerned. I guess this is kind of a breakup poem, too.

Franklin Pierce was the 14th President of the United States;
two before Lincoln. He died from alcoholism. I first visited
the "PIERCE MANSE" in 2011, on a Venture Grant from
Beloit College, where I travelled around New England to study
six of what I called "lesser-known presidents of the nineteenth
century." My tour guide at the Pierce Manse was an elementary
school teacher. She told me Pierce was a practical man: he saw
the poor quality of life experienced by freed slaves in New
Hampshire and knew that emancipation wasn't the answer,
that their lives were better as slaves, not everybody was mean
to them, and bad landowners spoiled it for everybody else. I
visited again during the summer of 2020, thanks to funding
from the Mastheads residency. The Manse was closed because
its staff were all old and at high risk for Covid-19. I love
studying the Civil War. Gertrude Stein wrote, "There never will
be anything more interesting in America than that Civil War
never."

Sharon Olds told me to write "ABOUT LBJ'S PENIS" at a
cocktail party at the Lillian Vernon Creative Writers House in
the West Village, where I got my MFA. When I heard this Yung
Miami line in "Take Yo Man" by City Girls: "Pussy ho, where
your man at? So I can fuck him in his mouth, in your house,
where he layin' at," I realized I should write more like that. More
confidently. Like, I deserve to brag, too. This poem originally
appeared in *The Yale Review*.

MISC. DEBTS: My teachers: at the Greater Hartford

Academy of the Arts: Christine Palm, Rafael Oses, Ben Zura, Will Hines (who showed me my first Lucille Clifton poem, changing my life forever), Pam Nomura; at Beloit College: Fran Abbate, Beatrice McKenzie, Jill Budny, Steve Wright; and at NYU: Rachel Zucker, Meghan O'Rourke, Terrance Hayes, Deborah Landau, Nick Laird!!!!!! My peers, my favorite writers: Jameson Fitzpatrick for pushing me to do all of this, Peach Kander, imogen xtian smith, Marti Irving, Claire Luchette, Dotun Akintoye, Kendra Allen, Chessy Normile, Monica Martin, Rachelle Toarmino, everyone in my MFA classes except the people I didn't like, and on and on and on. My bangs, Anna Sisson and Pete Baisden. Colleen and Owen, for making art with me. Brooke Sutter, who is a genius. Michael Doyle Olson, who is also a genius. Anyone who had to be my roommate in my twenties but especially Jenna Delesha and Emily Verburg. *The Round Table* staff but especially Megan, Bert, and Ian. All the Neigels, for being my family away from family and always taking care of me. My muses, all my boyfriends, whether they were my boyfriend or not. If we ever got drunk at the Crystal together on a Sunday night. Anyone who ever smoked me up or bummed me a cig. Nick and Mitch. Amy Winehouse, wherever you are. Dane Arts. My co-workers at Willalby's, Diner, Morris Ramen, and Underground Butcher: Dan, Justina, Jon, Ryan, I learned so much from you, I'm sorry I was drunk all the time. Katie Cacouris, who is perfect. Jill Bialosky, for all of this. Rachael Allen, for all of this and more and more and more—you reading my poems is the best thing that ever happened to me. My students, who are also my favorite writers. My family! My archangel, Aunt Ar. To the girl reading this <3.

I've always wanted to write a poem about Diane Nash, but I never have. Diane Nash, Freedom Rider, writing her will, just in case. Diane Nash, pregnant in jail. Diane Nash, almost ready to kill for those four little girls in Birmingham. I always think about how plantation cookbooks still smell like the kitchens they came from. I always hear Baraka: "Who are you, listening to me, who are you listening to yourself?" I'm on Roosevelt

Island crouching in a ball next to the giant FDR head. His head is triple the size of my body. I'm too close to him, and the security guard yells. I'm on a hill in a cemetery in Wisconsin, at the grave of one of Sally Hemmings' sons. I'm standing next to someone who will become my best friend, but neither of us know it yet. Who am I, listening to you, who am I listening to myself?

You're going to become a lot of things you don't know yet. No rice cakes, no cottage cheese, no individualism.

This book is printed with plant-based inks on materials certified by the Forest Stewardship Council®. The FSC® promotes an ecologically, socially and economically responsible management of the world's forests. This book has been printed without the use of plastic-based coatings.

The authorised representative in the EEA is eucomply OÜ, Pärnu mnt 139b-14, 11317 Tallinn, Estonia.
hello@eucompliancepartner.com
Tel. +33757690241